approaches to a
theology of history

approaches to a
theology
of history

by T. G. CHIFFLOT, O.P.

translated from the French by Mary Perkins Ryan

DESCLEE COMPANY   *New York - Tournai - Paris - Rome*

Originally published in French under the title
Approches d'une Théologie de l'Histoire
(Les Editions du Cerf, Paris 1960)

NIHIL OBSTAT

Gall Higgins, O. F. M. Cap.
Censor Librorum

IMPRIMATUR

✝ Terence J. Cooke, V. G.
New York, October 15, 1965

Library of Congress Catalog Card Number : 66-13369

Printed in Belgium

Contents

FOREWORD 3

Chapter I: CHRIST AND TIME 5

The liturgy and time 5

The "meaning of history" ... 6

The Christian idea of time ... 11

"Economy" and historical dialectic 25

"Economy" and "theology" ... 30

Conclusions 39

Chapter II: ESCHATOLOGY AS A FINE ART 41

When the "intransigent" is
fashionable 41

The kingdom of God and the
world 44

The world in the Christian perspective 47

The Good News proclaimed to
the world 54

And the profane world? 58

Chapter III: ST. THOMAS AQUINAS AND HIS-
TORY   61

History and its mystery   63

St. Thomas Aquinas, master of
the theology of history?   ...   73

Thomistic thought in the con-
text of its own history   75

The Thomistic synthesis and
history   77

Chapter IV: TOWARD A CHRISTIAN VISION OF
HISTORY   91

From the "Summit" to the
"Omega Point"   91

*Is the History of Man a Chapter in
the History of Nature?*   93

The history of man in the development of the world   93

The omega point   96

Consequences for Christian action   97

Man and His History   99

Toward a critical study   99

Maxwell's demon   101

Ivan and Alyosha   104

God Himself is historical as well
as eternal   108

Quasi non utentes   109

Foreword

In this book, four studies are brought together which appeared in different reviews (as noted at the beginning of each chapter). It seemed desirable to publish them in book form since their themes are closely related and their conclusions converge. In collecting them all under one cover, the author hopes to bring out more clearly whatever is of value in each. As he sees them, they constitute, not a complete study of the subject—for which he has neither the competence nor the leisure time necessary—but so many "approaches" to a problem with which theological thought is greatly concerned today: that of the "meaning of history."

The four essays presented here were all occasioned by previous publications. They do not form stages in an autonomous construction, but critical reflections on the thinking of four authors of very different mentalities and fields of specialization: Oscar Cullmann, Louis Bouyer, M. D. Chenu, and Teilhard de Chardin. This dependence on the thought of others puts an author's own merits, if any, in their proper perspective; the present author is quite willing to recognize himself as a rival of the Abbé Trublet satirized by Voltaire:

> The good man who has few brains
> can supplement them with someone else's.

But what may be no recommendation for an author may still be a recommendation for his work. The reader may perhaps benefit by the confrontation about an imaginary "round table"—brought about by a moderator who may be somewhat indiscreet— of these original, vital and contrasting views, the differences and the similarities between them being equally instructive. The author will have attained his purpose if he succeeds in making them better known.

CHAPTER I

Christus and time*

THE LITURGY AND TIME

The liturgy is bound up with time and opens out on
eternity. It is bound up with time in many ways.
The weekly recurrence of the day of the Lord, the
canonical hours, the cycle of the liturgical year, all
cause it to enter into the cyclic rhythm of *physical
time*. Again, the community gathered together to
celebrate the liturgy, the Church, lives in *historical
time*, the work of man. The liturgy bears the
marks, superficial or deep, of the individuals and the
generations who brought their different preoccupations to it, the mark of the cultural development of
which the people of God is the conveyor or the
author. Finally, more deeply, the liturgy exists in
relation to the *time of salvation*, because it recalls for
each generation the unique mystery of Christ, who
was crucified under Pontius Pilate, who rose again,
and who will return. [1]

* These reflections first appeared in *La Maison Dieu*, No. 13
(1948).
[1] See, for example, L. Bouyer, *The Paschal Mystery* (Chicago:
Regnery, 1950); O. Casel, *The Mystery of Christian Worship*
(Westminster: Newman, 1962).

This last and mysterious relationship, which claims to be neither a mere memory nor a mere expectation to an event of the past and to an event of the future, transcends the possibilities of the present. It presupposes that Christ is "now," at the very instant in which the liturgy is being celebrated, enthroned at the right hand of God; and so the time of the liturgy in some way encounters the eternity of God.

Thus, the liturgy and time poses a problem for theological thought. A remarkable book by Oscar Cullmann, entitled *Christ and Time*,[2] has formulated this problem in a new and suggestive way.

Indeed, this book not only makes a most important contribution to the traditional study of "the concept of time and of history in primitive Christianity," but also sheds a singularly pervasive light on several current debates which go beyond the field of liturgical research in the strict sense. We shall try to describe these debates briefly before going on to analyze Cullmann's book. The liturgical study of time will benefit, we believe, from being pursued in this wide context.

THE "MEANING OF HISTORY"

In the realm of thought, the nineteenth century has given us the idea of the "meaning of history." This now commonplace phrase requires some clarifica-

[2] Oscar Cullmann, *Christ and Time* (Westminster Press, 1950).

tion.   It is a fact that the works of the last century
have led to a perfecting of the "historical method,"
the scientific advantages of which are no longer
contested. [3]   But we must not misunderstand its
scope.   It puts us in possession of more accurate
means of knowing the past; it gives us the "sense
of the context," and obliges us to take time into
account in defining and judging doctrines.   But the
historical method does not modify the order of
thought itself nor call into question, on its own, the
atemporal character of the acquisitions of the mind:
a Harnack could claim, when all was said and done,
to disengage the "essence" of Christianity.

It is not the above but another manifestation of
the "meaning of history" which has caused time to
enter in a much more radical way into the intellectual
life of man.   Its origins and developments are many
and complex.   Since we are concerned here more
with raising problems than with solving them or
even stating them precisely, we shall describe these
problems briefly, although we are aware of the
inadequacy of such a presentation.

Classical thought, heir of the Greeks and, in
certain respects, of the Middle Ages and the
Renaissance, examined a world of *objects*.   The ideal
of knowledge was to contemplate "ideas" or at
least the order of "natures"—an order that was

---

[3] The historical method, freed of the abuses which
compromised it during the modernist controversies, has been
recommended and even commanded for both the study of the
Bible and of Christian origins (see the encyclical *Divino afflante
Spiritu*).

invariable and necessary, disengaged from time by abstraction—and to formulate eternal truths about them. Now, when a Kierkegaard speaks of "a truth that will be a truth *for me,*" it is precisely the objective and "eternal" truth that is being questioned. The knowing subject comes to enter into the very definition of truth. *"Objective uncertainty strongly appropriated by the most impassioned interiority, this is truth, the highest truth that there can be for an existing subject."*[4] This seems to constitute the decisive irruption of the "notion of history" into the life of the mind, for if "existence" enters into the definition of truth, time enters with it. But what kind of time?

It might be—as with Kierkegaard himself—the time of "interiority." We know how little use Kierkegaard had for world history: the only important thing, for the individual that I am, is the moment in which I am living (and, perhaps, the moment of eternity); the whole problem of time consists in the "repetition" of the moment. From Kierkegaard to contemporary existentialism, a whole current of thought regards time as above all a category of liberty determined by the free acts of man (and, if Christian perspectives are opened, the free intervention of God).

Others refuse to separate human existence from "history," that is, from the world in the process of development which surrounds it. If

[4] S. Kierkegaard, *Concluding Unscientific Postscript to Philosophic Fragments* (Princeton: Princeton U. Press, 1941).

truth, for Hegel and for Marx, is no longer identified with the atemporal idea, neither is it identified with individual subjectivity. It is to be sought "dialectically" in the total process of development of man and of the world. It is therefore profoundly within time, and time itself is not so much traversed by the unforeseeable interplay of human and divine free acts as organized from within into "moments" of this dialectic immanent in history.

These different aspects of modern thought have not remained, as we know, mere chapters in the history of philosophy. Each of them is the rendition of a concept of man, nourished by the concrete experience of a particular historical environment and situation, and reacting in turn on the ethical behavior of this environment. And so these aspects of modern thought cannot remain a matter of indifference to Christian thought, chiefly because the latter, while it has sometimes seemed a closed system of eternal truth, nonetheless has always acknowledged, in the very center of its Credo, its dependence on history. It can even claim, from many aspects, to have fathered this modern sense of history; its tradition contains many prefigures of it. It is therefore not surprising that the modern preoccupation with time, in its various forms, finds an echo in theology.

When Kierkegaard gives the definition of truth quoted above, he immediately notes that this definition is "a transcription of that of faith." [5]

[5] *Ibid.*

Before him, St. Augustine had given—in quite different philosophical categories—a definition of truth and of conversion to truth which is no less "interior": "Do not go outside yourself, return within yourself; truth dwells in man's interiority." [6] A whole current of Christian thought, one that has never run dry and gushes forth abundantly in our day, tends to apprehend Christian truth as grasped in an interior history and to measure time by the events of this history, that is, by eternity (but the eternity of the living God and not that of the "eternal verities"). The whole history of salvation itself is considered above all in its supra-temporal implications, the unforeseeable interruptions of the divine transcendence in time.

But other Christian themes are mingled with this one. St. Augustine, in *The City of God*, brings out the idea of a Church journeying through time, in the perspective of world and even cosmic history which Kierkegaard refused to see. This idea is also among those which are profoundly in harmony with today's Christian mentality. Certain thinkers admit willingly that the "continued Incarnation," or "Jesus Christ poured out and communicated" in a sense not foreseen by Bossuet, grows by taking on the moments of a historical dialectic, of a maturation of the world in which the "pleroma" of Christ is being organically prepared within time itself.

Time of freedom and of transcendence, time of

[6] *De vera religione* XXXIX, 72.

world history and of cosmic development—it is easy to see how these different conceptions of time imply different positions with regard to the Christian mystery, especially the liturgical mystery, and also with regard to this world. These positions confront one another today in Christian thought and in Christian action. But in its fundamental data, before any intellectual elaboration, Revelation contains some basic statements about time. These can and should serve as a touchstone today. To discover them and then, from them, to lay out as it were the theological specifications for any Christian conception of time—this is the task which the work of Oscar Cullmann invites us to undertake, the work which we must now analyze.

THE CHRISTIAN IDEA OF TIME

The Christian conception of time, according to the authors of the New Testament, is essentially characterized, in Cullmann's analysis, by two marks: on the one hand, the events of Revelation and salvation are located along a continuous and ascending line, a dynamic relationship of development *(oikonomia)* exists between them; on the other hand, each of these events—and in the first place the central and decisive event of the series, the event of the Pasch—is grasped in its historical uniqueness *(Einmaligkeit)*, as having happened once and for all *(ephapax)*. The first two parts of the book bring out in the richest and most coherent way the meaning of these two New Testament terms: *oikonomia* and *ephapax*.

1.   The "economy" of salvation implies, in the New Testament writings, the most "naïve" and the most strongly realistic idea of time.   While Plato's time, that "moving image of eternity," and the time of the Greeks in general, found its most adequate image in the closed circle, it is the infinitely extended straight line which represents Christian and Judaic time.   Along this line are located human "times" *(kairoi)*: those which man chooses for his action and those which God determines.   Like man, God has His "D-Days," and those of God are not those of man (cf. Jn 7, 6), though these two are located in the same linear continuum, and not outside time in any atemporal beyond.   "Times" divide time; the *kairoi* define, in the indefinite extension of duration, the *aiones*, the periods which are at once those of time and those of eternity. There is an *aion autos*, a "present age," reaching from the day of creation to the day of the "end of times"; there is an *aion* before creation (designated by the expression *ek tou aionos*); there is an *aion mellon*, an age to come, after the end of times; and the *aiones ton aionon*, the "ages of ages," which include the whole of this duration, are also coextensive with the eternity of God.

But if the divine "eternity" itself is thus "naïvely" conceived as the indefinite extension of time, its transcendence is manifested in the fact that God is the Lord of time.   This lordship is

affirmed in many ways.   For God "a thousand years
are as one day" (2 Pt 3, 8), and where God acts, the
frontiers of the ages are bridged; all things pre-exist
in Him; Christ, even though He also did not know
"the day and the hour," is nonetheless the bearer
and the agent of this mastery, His action anticipates
the age to come.   In the Church, this "eschatological
element" is already at work and, by the celebration
of the Eucharist, the whole temporal line of salvation
is, as it were, concentrated in one "day of the Lord"
which at once recalls the historical day of Easter
and proclaims that of the Parousia.   Finally, the life
of the Christian in the Spirit renders him also a
participant both in the whole history of salvation
and in the effects that this history brings about in
temporal duration.

   But all these manifestations of the lordship of
God over time only develop the consequences of His
principal intervention in temporal duration, that is,
through Jesus Christ.   The result, for the Christian,
is a new division of time, the one which even our
way of dating events, before and after Jesus Christ,
translates into common usage.   For messianic
Judaism, the *center (Mitte)* of time, which gives it
its decisive orientation, is the *end* of *times*.   For
Christianity, this center is a fact of the *past*, the event
of which Christ is the subject and Easter the decisive
moment.   Henceforth, for the Christian, on the
threefold division of time—time before creation,
"the present age," and "the age to come"—is
superimposed a twofold division, of which Easter
is the dividing line.   Because of this, the period that

extends from Easter to the end of the world takes on apparently contradictory characteristics. It still belongs to the "present age," but the "age to come" has already virtually begun in it, since the decisive instant from which this age to come proceeds is no longer to be awaited, it has already happened. The Parousia is "V Day," and the war is not finished; but the decisive battle has already taken place. After the decisive day and before the definitive day, we are in the "last times"—however long they may go on.

Cullmann here takes a position against the "consistent eschatology" which constituted the essence of primitive faith for Albert Schweitzer and Martin Werner. They are most likely right in insisting on the fact that Christian salvation is linked with time, and in insisting on the eschatological hope of the first Christians. But they have not seen that this hope which, as they describe it, was already that of Judaism, is henceforth, since the first Easter, based on faith in an event *of the past*. The fact that the last days have been prolonged does not change their character. To suppose that the end was *close at hand*, even admitting that the first Christians or Jesus Himself ventured to do so, was only a psychological error in perspective without any theological consequences.

The event of Easter is, therefore, in every respect, the event which is the "midpoint," the center toward which all previous history tends and from which all later history flows. It is in their relation to this central moment that all times are organized in an economy, constituting, with their *kairoi*, an ascending line, a *Heilslinie* which is a *Christuslinie*. New Testament texts flow from Cullmann's pen stating this Christological perspective as applied to the whole of history—including what escapes the "history" of the historian: creation and the end of time.   The whole process of cosmic and human development is thus included, and the perspective narrows at first—from the whole of creation to mankind summed up in Adam, from mankind to the chosen people to its "remnant," from the remnant to the unique Servant of Yahweh—only to widen out anew from Christ to the Twelve, from these to the Church and from the Church to all men whom she calls, and even to the "new heavens" and the "new earth" when "God will be all in all."   The choice (election) which sets apart, in the general development of the world, a more and more limited segment in whom the history of salvation is played out, is a choice of representation *(Stellvertretung)* in which the element chosen—and, finally, Christ—is the bearer of the destiny of all the others.

2.   If all the moments of the history of salvation are thus brought together in one perspective, in one single *oikonomia*, we must beware of making them into so many "dialectic moments" the reality of which would be above all that of an atemporal idea developing through them, or again of reducing them to the successive appearances of an ideal myth. They are, on the contrary, strictly temporal, and this is the first meaning of the *ephapax* which the

New Testament uses in abundance, the content of this term being explained in the second part of Cullmann's book. *Ephapax* means to have taken place "once," with all the triteness, all the opaqueness of a *fact*. But also in the second sense of the word, inseparable from the first, it is to have happened "once for all." The event which is completely immersed in the unfolding of temporal duration is nevertheless definitive; it has a decisive importance *for all times*.

This historical uniqueness, this *Einmaligkeit*, characterizes above all the whole event of which Christ is the subject. If the remoteness in history between us and the Gospel accounts blurs their reality for us, if its geographical distance causes us to idealize the "Holy Land," if the Cross itself has become a sacred theme, the first Christian generations had, by contrast, a very clear estimation of the scandal of seeing this very banal fact: that Jesus of Nazareth had been nailed to a cross, raised to the rank of the decisive event of history. The Jews were already scandalized to learn that the Messias was from Nazareth, and the insistence of St. Paul on Christ crucified directly offended them. The temptation to minimize the scandal led to the great Christian heresy, Docetism—Docetism in the strict sense, as in the gnosis of Basilides or the heresy of Cerinthus who refused to identify the Messias with the Crucified; but Docetism also in the Christological controversies, inasmuch as the redeeming work of Christ was forgotten in polemicizing about His two natures. Cullmann here quotes Melanchthon: *"Hoc est Christus cognoscere, beneficia ejus cognoscere, non quod isti docent ejus naturas, modos incarnationis contueri."* "To know Christ means to know His deeds for our benefit and not, as these people teach, to reflect on His natures, the modes of His Incarnation." To devote oneself, in respect to the history of salvation, to speculation is, according to this author, to abandon the perspective of the New Testament.

Like the actions of Christ, the events of salvation before and after Christ are events that take place once, *ephapax.* The *past* of the Old Testament retains all its temporal distance with regard to the Christ for whom it prepares, and this is why Cullmann denies the validity of the allegorical method, which unduly does away with this distance.

In the same way, the eschatological future retains the temporal character of a future event. It is no longer necessary to insist on this.

But we must insist, rather, on this portion of the time after Christ which is our present, that is, the time between the Ascension and the Parousia in which Christians are living. From its particular relation to the center and to the end of time, this time receives a new significance, which is, as Cullmann sees it, the touchstone of fidelity to the New Testament message. The pages which he devotes to it, rich in a theology of faith, in an eschatology, in a theology of the liturgy, are marvelously solid.

The primitive community, he tells us, has the most vivid awareness of the present, the sense of living in a time necessary to the history of salvation. But, on the contrary, when we refer the acts of the Christian life to eternity, we make this life banal and commonplace, losing the sense of the New Testament *ephapax*.

The decisive consideration here is a "dialectical" one, but this is a dialectic of *times* and not of ideas. The present time is not, according to the New Testament, subject to the tension between time and eternity, but to this other tension we have already noted in analyzing the Christian divisions of time: the tension between the two *aiones*, the present age and the age to come, to both of which the present time belongs simultaneously. From this tension flow all the characteristics of the present in the history of salvation.

What is happening "at present?" Christ, who rose from the dead and who will come again, is now reigning. He reigns over all things in heaven and on earth, and on earth the center of His reign is the Church, the "body" of Christ. The time of the Church is essentially the time of Christ's reign, and the temporal tension that characterizes the reign of Christ, between His Ascension and His return, also makes its mark on the life of the Church. The Church, like Christ ascended into heaven, lives "between times." And this explains the seeming contradictions of its being.

Thus, for example, both sin and sanctity accompany the Church from its very beginnings. For the Spirit, the "element of the end of time," and the flesh, still of this age, are simultaneously

at work in the Church, which shares in the two
"ages."   Thus again, in the Eucharistic synaxis,
the faith of Christians sees the past and the future
together.   The presence in our midst of Christ
who is reigning implies both the memory of His
Resurrection[7] and the expectation of His return.
"At the Supper, the situation of the present time in
the history of salvation *(heilsgeschichtlich)* is concre-
tized, so to say, in its totality: its close and
simultaneous relationship to the center and to the
end of time."

And so, finally, the task proper to the Church,
the missionary proclamation of the Gospel, is
assigned to her by reason of her situation in the
"between time."   The proclamation of the Gospel is,
for the Church, at once the sign which heralds the
end of times (when all people have been evangelized,
"the end will come") and the duty incumbent upon
her to hasten this end.   In this missionary task
resides the proper significance of the present, its
meaning *(Sinn)* in the history of salvation.   "It is
the *ephapax* of the present time."

Cullmann succeeds in clarifying his thoughts on
the time of the Church by locating it in relation to
two opposed concepts which he judges erroneous,
that of Kierkegaard and that of Catholicism.   Both

---

[7] Of His Resurrection and not primarily of His Passion.
For Cullmann (cf. *Early Christian Worship* [Chicago: Regnery, 1953]),
the Eucharistic assembly on the Lord's Day recalls first of all the
meals of the Risen Lord with His disciples, and it is only under
the influence of St. Paul (I Cor 11) that the memory of the Last
Supper, always there from the beginning, but in the background,
supplants the former.

go astray on the same point: the temporal distance from the Church's present to Christ's past, a distance which both pretend to do away with. Kierkegaard does so by forgetting the present: for him, faith renders the believer contemporary with Christ; it removes from history the relationship of the Christian to salvation. Affirming the necessity for a "leap" over time, Kierkegaard forgets the basic statement of the New Testament: Christ is now reigning. The Catholic Church, at the other extreme, pretends to lay hold of this Christ in the present, as if His present reign did not have to be referred to the past event of Easter. She annuls the *ephapax* of the Redemption by detaching it from the one time in which it is located and making it her present treasure. Catholicism makes of the present, of the time of the Church, an absolute *(Verabsolutierung der Gegenwart)*. According to Cullman, the Paschal *ephapax* is rendered present *(vergegenwärtigt)* to the Church, just as with Kierkegaard the Christian becomes a contemporary of Christ. In both cases the temporal distance is abolished, the true character of the *ephapax* is misunderstood.

Cullmann therefore denies the Catholic theology of the Mass as being the re-presentation *(Vergegenwärtigung)* of the Passion: for "He who now appears to the assembled community does *not* appear as crucified *(gekreuzigt Werdender)* and rising again, nor as coming again for the eschatological Parousia, but as seated at the right hand of God, He who was crucified and has risen and will come again. As such, He now grants the forgiveness of sins which He effected in the past and promises the consummation which He will bring."

He equally denies the Catholic idea of tradition. It forgets the decisive and normative character of the *ephapax* effected in Christ; it forgets most particularly the unique character of the apostolic times which are, as it were, welded to the times of the Gospel: "The foundation is only laid once."

We shall return to these controversial points. For the present we shall merely note that if Cullmann thinks he must maintain the unique normative value of the past against Catholicism, he does not any the less maintain, against a "narrow Protestantism," the proper value of the time of the Church in the history of salvation.

The two veins that we have just followed with Cullmann— *oikonomia, ephapax*—have allowed the author to define the Christian concept of time. The last two parts of the book make certain consequences clear. We shall dwell on them at less length, in spite of their interest.

3.   The third part describes the relationships of the history of salvation to the general development of the world. For the history of salvation is not a thin thread among the others in the rich tapestry of general history. The world in its totality is not a stranger to the lordship of Christ. Christ is the mediator of creation; at the Parousia He will return all things to the Father. In the meantine, the confession, *"Kyrios Christos,"* implies a universal

reign. The privileged choice of Israel, of its "remnant," of the Messias, is only a substitution of a part for the whole, for the final benefit of the whole. Now that Christ has ascended into heaven, it is "time" for the pagans to reenter into the economy of this salvation that has been gained for them, so that God may be "all in all." This is the task of the Church, the "body" of the risen Christ: to call them into it as she expands to the ends of the earth. Thus the Church and the world are not juxtaposed, but, as it were, concentric, Christ being their center. Both belong to the domain of Christ, and the Church, which knows this, must tell it to the world that does not know it.

As to the powers of this world—the *exousia* of Rom 13 and the *archontes* of 1 Cor 2, 8, which stand, as Cullmann sees it, for both the civil powers of the Roman world and the spiritual powers which act through them—they give witness in their own way to the ambiguous and dialectic character of this "between time" which is the time of the Church. For they are, here and now, subject to the reign of Christ who has "subjected all things under His feet," and yet they retain a certain liberty until the end of time, their hostility finally serving the Kingdom. This dualism—which is not metaphysical but, to repeat, temporal—rules the complex attitude of the Christian toward the state. Subjected to the reign of Christ, these powers carry out the will of God according to the order fixed by Him: and so we have the positive recommendations of respect and obedience given in Rom 13. But hostile to this reign, they call for the Christian's defiance and become, in his eyes, the "Beast."

Is the Christian, then, finally to accept or refuse the world? The proper situation of the present time in the history of salvation and the complex relationships of the world to the reign of Christ call for the equally complex response of 1 Cor 7, 31: "to use the world as if not using it."

4. The fourth part of the book studies the place and role of the *individual* in the history of salvation. Christianity, more than any other concept of man, insists on the unique value of personal destiny. How can this insistence be reconciled with the affirmation of a collective "economy" of salvation?

These do not have to be reconciled, for they refer to the *same* reality. The history of salvation, in all these phases, concerns each Christian. *Tua res agitur.* "If you have risen with Christ, seek the things that are above, where Christ is seated at the right hand of God... You are dead, and your life is hidden with Christ in God. When Christ, your life, shall appear, then you too will appear with Him in glory" (Col 3, 1-4). This whole history is therefore my own.

The past is *my* past. I am dead and risen again "with" Christ. Here again Cullmann refuses to conceive the Paulinian *syn* in a mystical sense, that of a presence *(Vergegenwärtigung)* of the Paschal mystery to the Christian. The only link between this past and present is faith, by which I grasp that this past has been accomplished for me. It implies the divine election, by which I belong, from the beginning, to the economy of salvation.

For the individual Christian, the present is first of all the *gift of the Spirit*, given to him according to his own measure, but for the sake of the Church, causing him thus to enter as an irreplaceable element into the actual developing process of salvation. It is then the *commandment of God* to which the New Testament demands of the Christian an inventive and free obedience. For the New Testament adds nothing to the imperatives of the Old except as an "indicative": "the time has come" when the law must be "fulfilled." The attitude of Jesus with regard to the law as well as His moral prescriptions, all connected with the evaluation of the new circumstances, and His parables in which He Himself creates and describes the circumstances which demand a certain way of behaving—all these manifest the freedom of judgment and the concrete attention to the times with which the Christian ought to act.

Paul does the same. There exists only one principle of general application: love. But the imperative of love is also based upon an "indicative," that of the love God has shown us. Thus, the whole ethic of the New Testament is also *"heilsgeschicht-lich."*

The future of the individual Christian is also closely bound up with the history of salvation. There is no personal destiny outside the perspective of the end of time, because, for man, there is no *natural* survival after death. In order that life may come from death, there must be a creative miracle on God's part, the very miracle accomplished at Easter in Christ, which miracle is to be extended at the end of time to all those who sleep "in Him." The hope of the individual Christian is, therefore, hope in the *final* resurrection. But the Judaic hope in the resurrection, founded on faith in God the Creator, is henceforth founded on faith in the Resurrection of Christ. Christ rose in the past and now lives by the Spirit. This same Spirit is given to us, He is the pledge in our mortal bodies of the resurrection to come. To die, before the Parousia, is "to be with Christ," to enter into the closest possession of the same pledge, and those who are dead "in the Lord" still have ahead of them the future of the resurrection. Thus we again find, in the attitude of the Christian toward his destiny, the tension characteristic of the present time between the past and the future: "God has saved us *and* will save us from death" (2 Cor 1, 10).

"ECONOMY" AND HISTORICAL DIALECTIC

The work that we have just analyzed rests on a critical exegesis of the New Testament extended in biblical theology. Leaving to better qualified scholars the task of examining its exegetical bases, which as a whole, *salvo meliori judicio*, we accept as such, we shall devote ourselves here to its theological aspect; and it is on this level that, having stated our agreement with its essence, we shall formulate some important reservations.   The reader should not assume from this that, in judging the conclusions of an exegete, we are going to look for a criterion outside of New Testament revelation. On the contrary, it is the New Testament itself, as Cullmann helps us to read it, which, in our opinion, does not lend itself to certain of his conclusions.

But we must first point out what we believe to be the indisputable and helpful contribution of this book to contemporary theology: the vigorous realism of the New Testament notion of time. The ease—the sign of rare mastery—with which Cullmann cites, in connection with each debatable issue, the texts in point, and the sure touch with which, respecting their context, he extracts their true, authentic, and rich essence, carry a conviction which grows stronger and clearer with each page: Christianity is not a philosophy of history, it is not even a theology of history; it is first of all, in the simplest sense of the word, a *history*.   Time thus plays an essential role in it, but it is the time of history, not the time of philosophical speculation. His New Testament notion of time is therefore at once very inclusive and very rich because it is so temporal.   The past, the present, and the future again find their distances, their irreversibility and their unexpectedness.   The events of salvation are truly events; they give us the mystery of God with all the authority, even the harsh reality of the *fait accompli*.

Time, consequently, is not the mythical context from which we must disengage *(entmythologisieren)* the atemporal kernel *(Kern)* of Christian beliefs. (Here Cullmann takes a very firm stand against Bultmann.) Nor is it reducible to an idea which would prescribe its real unfolding. In this respect, the "naïvely linear" biblical outline—here opposed to the cyclical time of the Greeks, itself the image of unmoving eternity—is no less opposed to any explanation of the "dialectical" sort, according to which the idea, no longer unchangeable in its necessity but immanent to the process of becoming, would make time into a logical entity. Time remains honestly temporal. And, finally, time does not disappear before eternity, and the event of salvation is not "the irruption of eternity into time," if we understand by this expression that time now loses all its proper value, that it is depreciated *(banalisé)*. Cullmann's opposition to Kierkegaard and even to Karl Barth on this point is pregnant with meaning.

Let us return to the two key words of the Christian doctrine of time, *oikonomia* and *ephapax*. If our analysis has been fairly faithful, the reader has already grasped how far these terms, in spite of their theological condensation, remain authentically temporal. The "economy" is not a dialectic, for if it affirms God's mastery ordering the totality of time, it eliminates neither temporal distances nor the newness of each of its moments, nor the unpredictable freedom of each of the actions which constitute it. The Old Testament recounts the preparations for the Gospel: it is not a crypto-grammic pre-Gospel in which the Gospel itself would be contained. The tension between the present and the future, the "already ended" and the "not yet achieved," which characterizes the time of the Church and "gives the key to the whole New Testament," is not a "metaphysical" tension; it is rooted in the temporal distance between the event of Easter and that of the Parousia. Between the two, time is "shortened" but not suppressed.

If the *oikonomia* is not a dialectical entity, neither is the New Testament *ephapax* a myth or a temporal foretaste of eternity; it is an event. The pages in which Cullmann, against all types of "Docetism," revives the scandal of the Cross, that is, that the "mystery" is first of all an "actual fact," retain all their value, even if one does not agree with the author that the acceptance of the actual fact must forbid all contemplation of, and even all speculation on the mystery.

In the same way, Cullmann's insistence on reminding the Christian that he is not living in eternity but also in an *ephapax* which is an irreplaceable present, seems to us particularly timely. This analysis of the "time of the Church"—whatever the reservations we are about to make—brings with it a threefold teaching to which we must completely subscribe. First, this time is defined, for the use of the Christians who are living in it, by its situation between an event of the past, Easter, and an event of the future, the Parousia. In the second place, neither the past resurrection of Christ nor His future return could thus radically affect the present time separating them if the same Christ who rose again and who will come were not, *at this very moment*, living and reigning. Finally, this time is the time of the Church, as far as the whole world is concerned, but it is also the time of *each* Christian, who by his personal election is given the whole history of salvation as his own history.

In this connection it would be instructive to draw a parallel between Christian man and Marxist man, in their respective situations with regard to history. The Marxist believes, explicitly or not, that he is living with time and progressing with history. The revolution as he sees it is projecting itself into the temporal future, and one or another stage of the revolution can serve to mark out the past. But what is his *present* bond with this future and this past? For him the present is the "objective situation," the overall phenomenon of the class war, or again the present condition of socialist progress. Between him and this situation, there is the material bond of his belonging to it economically, a bond he must be aware of in order to be the active agent (whether deterministically or freely is another question) of the revolutionary process; between this present situation and the future revolution is the "historical dialectic." Between Marxist man and the revolution, there thus exists a double mediation, at once logical and material, both becoming conscious in him: that which binds the individual to the mass and that which binds the present to the future. It is through these bonds that the Marxist man is "in the meaning of history." Christian man on the contrary—whatever his position with regard to socialism—if he is in the Church, is so because of his personal and immediate faith in the Christ who chose him; if he remembers Easter and awaits the Parousia, it is because Christ is living now. The present life and reign of Christ, not a dialectic, connect the past and the future; the blood poured out "for me" makes this history *my* history. All intermediaries disappear: the Christian is "in the meaning of history" because and to the extent that he lives with the living God and reigns with Christ, who reigns over time.

"ECONOMY" AND "THEOLOGY"

Nonetheless, however widely we accept this radical temporality of the history of salvation, which Cullmann enables us to grasp in the New Testament, we must deny certain negative consequences which he draws from it. We trust that we have succeeded in making it clear that these reservations do not affect adherence to Cullmann's central message, but rather have no other intention than to safeguard it. We do not wish to disguise the fact that the points which we are going to discuss all lead us to the crucial issue of the controversy between Catholicism and Protestantism: the total Protestantism of the author and, on our part, various specifically Catholic theses are at stake here. Such a debate can only be fruitful if we carry it to its true center, which is also the place where we have a chance of truly meeting one another: the terrain of Revelation. Our divergences originate in a common desire to be faithful to this very Revelation; and from this flows the grave seriousness of the break that took place with the reform, dividing us at the very heart of our faith. But hope is also born from this: even if we cannot convince one another, a step will be taken toward unity and other steps made possible each time that we are able, in explaining ourselves, to give our mutual witness to this common desire for fidelity.

The first point concerns the divine eternity. Cullmann refuses to consider it outside of time *(zeitlos)*, since all that we know of God, His intervention in creation and redemption, are located in the course of time. *Aion* (an age) and *aiones* (the ages) always retain a temporal meaning. The perfect simultaneity of a nonsuccessive duration, as Catholic theology commonly defines the divine eternity, contradicts the New Testament which, under the term "eternity" *(aiones ton aiones)*, sees only the indefinite extension of time.

However, and Cullmann insists on this also, the revealed relationship of God to duration implies another element: the lordship of God over time. If God manifests Himself in time, and only in time, He manifests Himself sovereignly in time. The succession, the irreversibility, the mutual opaqueness of the various segments of duration raise no obstacle either to divine foreknowledge and predestination, or to this shortening of perspectives which the earthly presence of the Incarnate Word effects between the present time and the time to come, or to the action of the Spirit, the "element of the end of time," in the Christian and in the Church. The very image of the "decisive battle" which assures in advance the "V-Day" of sacred history, however enlightening it may be, should not deceive us: no earthly battle can be this decisive in advance. We must therefore recognize a radical "difference" in the relationship of God and of man with regard to time.   God alone reigns over time.

Thus, if God allows His interventions to be located in our duration (and it is certainly here that the New Testament lays hold of them), He does not allow them to be enclosed within it.   The relation of God to time (if we may use such an expression) escapes our definitions, for one of its terms escapes us: God in His mystery.   Revelation obliges us to recognize this mystery, and both Protestant and Catholictheology try to meet this obligation.

But it is precisely at this point that their rupture reveals itself.   I shall characterize them by two apparently similar expressions which nonetheless describe two profoundly different attitudes: "to pause in the presence of the mystery"; "to become aware of the mystery."   To pause in the presence of the mystery means, having encountered it, to accept it in the very terms in which it is stated: here, to juxtapose the intervention of God in our time and the reign of God over time; and to deny to thought any possibility of progress in knowledge.   To become aware of the mystery is certainly not to explain it and certainly not to reduce it to the categories of a philosophy, but, having accepted it by faith, to look at it in order to express it. *Fides quaerens intellectum.*

Here this regard believes it must try to seek in the very duration *of God* the secret of His intervention in *our* duration. The reign of God over time, the transcendence of God with regard to the laws of time manifested by His interventions, oblige us to state that God Himself is not temporal. His duration is of another order, and knows no succession, as ours does. If anything can be said about it, it is not Greek philosophy that will teach it to us. But it can help us to express what Revelation obliges us to admit.

Thus, to speculate on eternity may mean to be tempted to reduce the mystery of God to one of the things that can be arrived at by philosophy, to "Hellenize" Christianity. But it may also mean, in a formula like that given by Boethius to the meditations of Thomas Aquinas: "*Interminabilis vitae tota simul possessio,*" to seek to express the transcendence of God's duration in relation to our own, as we are obliged to admit this transcendence by the characteristics of the action of God on time given us in Revelation, and precisely in order to give them their full meaning. It is indeed, in this perspective, the very "linear" scheme of the New Testament that obliges us to see behind it the mystery of God that no scheme can express.

We can now touch more briefly, in spite of its importance, on a second point: Christology.

We find here the same tension between two series of revealed statements which cannot, as we see it, be maintained together except by recourse to the mystery and thus force us, beyond their immediate bearing, to formulate this mystery. The double significance of the *ephapax* applied to the event of which Christ is the subject sums them up. This event is temporal, it has happened "once" as any human act happens once. But it has happened "once for all" in a sense not found in any human act. We are here in the presence of the mystery of Christ. Here again, should we refrain from "speculation?" Yes, certainly, if this would, merely to satisfy the mind, mean doing away with the scandal of the temporality of salvation, as with Docetism—or if it would mean, as with liberalism, bringing the event back within the usual framework of history: that is, in both cases to abandon something of Revelation.

But is the Church following Docetism when, taking up the question of Mk 4, 41: "Who, then, is this man that the winds and the sea obey Him?," she has asked how the death of the carpenter of Nazareth could be the salvation of the world, and has tried to formulate the mystery of the natures of Christ in order to seal her faith in the mystery of salvation? The text of Melanchthon quoted by Cullmann—here again, in a topical way—seems to us characteristic of this pausing in the presence of the mystery, to which we believe that we must oppose—in the very name of the "obedience of faith"—becoming aware of the mystery. "*Modus incarnationis contueri*," to go back to the mystery of Christ, is to assure ourselves that we are faithful to faith in His Redemption: "*beneficia ejus cognoscere.*"

Whether we are concerned with eternity or Christology, we are brought back, as we have seen, to one and the same question, the solution of which includes the solutions of particular problems. It is basically a question of knowing whether soteriology, essential to faith, whether adherence to the salvation that comes from God, excludes, authorizes, or requires an act of knowing turned toward God Himself; in other words whether the *oikonomia* excludes, authorizes, or requires a *theologia*. We certainly recognize the danger of a theology that thinks it can find the means of knowing God elsewhere than in the concrete economy of His Revelation. The fear of this "*theologia gloriae*" is the beginning of a faithful theology. But we also believe that God reveals *Himself* by intervening in our history to make it the history of salvation and that there is no *true* "theology of the Cross" which is not, in the full sense of the word, "theology."

Naturally enough we encounter these two conceptions of theology—which imply two conceptions of the liturgy—when we touch on a third point: that of the Church's present and its relationship, in particular its Eucharistic relationship, with the past, with the event of the Redemption. Here again Cullmann makes it possible for us to grasp the precise problem. On the one hand, he insists on the temporal distances that separate the time of the Church from the resurrection and the return of Christ: to pretend to abolish these distances by projecting the events of salvation into eternity, or by making an absolute of the present moment in which these events encounter our faith, would be to deny the *ephapax* which is precisely the seal of their reality.   But, on the other hand, there exists between these distant events and the time of the Church a relationship which neither chronology nor the psychology of memory and anticipation can suffice to explain.   No other past, no other future exercise such dominion over the present.   If the time of the Church is so profoundly affected by its past and its future, it must be because the reality acquired by this past and promised for this future is contemporary with her.   In fact, the same Christ who is risen and who will return again is now reigning, seated at the right hand of God.

We are therefore constrained, once more, to state in temporal terms a mystery that seems to contradict time: the mystery of the Church.   And we already perceive its close relationship to the other two mysteries already recognized: that of the divinity of Christ and that of the divine eternity. We can, once again, simply pause in the presence of the mystery and merely juxtapose the declaration of the temporal distances and the statement that "at present Christ reigns."   We can also, having done this, realize that this grammatical present connects something other than time with time.   The reproaches that Cullmann addresses to the Catholic theology of the Church presuppose the first attitude.

They collapse if we find in the New Testament itself the necessity for choosing the second attitude.

Thus, if we interpret the "to die with Christ" of St. Paul in a mystical sense, by applying it to the baptism of the Christian, if we see in the Mass the Passion "rendered present," it may be because we misunderstand the *ephapax* of Rom 6, 10. But it may be because we confess in the present reign of the living Christ the double mystery of an entrance of Christ rising from the dead into the prerogatives of God, and of a divine eternity in which "a thousand years are as one day," that we do not assert the reign of man over the present and the absolute value of the present, but the divinity of Christ and the reign of God over time. In the same way, if we accept a living and normative tradition in the Church, it may be that we believe that we can prolong, beyond Scripture, a Revelation that has been given only once. But it may be that this Revelation, connected with time in its unique expression, appears as escaping time, not only because "what is written remains" but because the Spirit, "that element of the end of time," assists the Church to guard and understand what He has inspired.

The three preceding points: the doctrine of eternity, Christology, ecclesiology, flow from a theology that is properly Christian. One last point obliges us to enter into the difficult debate on "natural theology," and we can sketch this out only briefly.

Whether in connection with the Hellenic conception of cyclic time, or in connection with the history of the profane world *(Weltgeschichte)* and its autonomous development, particularly through the hostile activity of the *exousiai* and the *archontes tou kosmou*, Cullmann seems to reject or at least deliberately to ignore any possibility of an authentic communication between the Christian concept and any natural and profane concept of time and of history.

It seems to us that, here again, theological thought can and should go beyond the mere juxtaposition of the contrasted elements of the mystery (here, the mystery of creation in its relations with Redemption). To affirm, on the one hand, the proper, profane, and even hostile character of the realities of this world and of human history, their incapacity to prepare or even to call for the gratuitous event of the realities of salvation; to maintain, on the other hand, that there is nothing in the world and in human history which does not "live, move and have its being" in Christ—this can and, to our way of thinking, should lead us to seek in the created *nature* of things and of man, in the created dynamism that sustains their becoming, on this side of the sin that wounds nature and corrupts action and "subjects them to vanity," the ontological outlines of that *"expectatio creaturae"* spoken of in the Epistle to the Romans. To sketch out this process of thought and to show how cosmic becoming and human history certainly cannot introduce us to the history of salvation but can, on the contrary, in the light of that history, become an object of theological concern, will engage us later on. We hope to return to it at another point.

CONCLUSIONS

These reflections do not exhaust the rich content of Cullmann's book, nor the theological theme outlined in these words: Christ and time. But perhaps they will help us, by the light of the New Testament, to see more clearly into the debates now in progress between theologians of "eschatology" and theologians of "incarnation." It seems to us that the following conclusions may be retained:

1. The time of the Christian Revelation is not conceptual but concrete. Creation, Redemption, and the Parousia are events having real dates (whether their dates be known to us or not) and located on a continuous and irreversible line. Together they form a history.

2. The central event of Easter organizes this history, making it an "economy" in which each of the segments of the whole duration receives, from its situation before or after the "midpoint" of time, its proper significance.

3. The unique event of Easter receives this decisive and normative character with regard to all times from Him who is its subject, Christ. The

Incarnation affirms within time the lordship of God over time.

4. To state this lordship is to recognize the transcendence of God Himself in relation to time (eternity). It is also to confess that the risen Christ participates in this transcendence, retaining in the present period of His reign the efficacy of His past Passion and anticipating the virtue of His return to come. Thus, the concrete historicity of salvation reveals in time a mystery that transcends time, and our adhesion to the *oikonomia* calls for a *theologia*.

5. Faith and the sacraments together constitute this adhesion to the historical *oikonomia* and this *theologia*. They cause the Church and the Christian, who live within time, to participate in the reign of Christ over time.

6. The study of the relationships between the history of salvation and the general becoming of the world should do justice, on the one hand, to the transcendence and to the gratuity of the *redemptive* intervention of God; on the other hand, to the absolute dependence, with the exception of sin, of everything that is and is becoming on the *creative* action of God in Christ.

CHAPTER II

Eschatology as a fine art *

WHEN THE "INTRANSIGENT" IS FASHIONABLE

If I allow myself (and if the editors and Fr. Bouyer himself allow me) to take exception here to several important points in his article *Christianisme et Eschatologie*, it is first of all because the conclusions of the author on these points seem to me to be open to discussion. But it is also because, as I see it, a discussion of these points of disagreement may put us on guard against a danger: that of agreeing with Fr. Bouyer on the very points where there is no call for discussion, not so much because of the truth of what he says as because of the attractiveness of extreme attitudes—an attractiveness felt by many people. For my own part, I refuse to identify this attraction with the thirst for the absolute, still less with the true intransigence of the faith. It can be the expression of these values, but it can also

* This article appeared in *La Vie Intellectuelle* of October, 1948, in answer to Fr. Bouyer's article, "Christianisme et Eschatologie." Nevertheless, it seemed to me that my text could be presented by itself, omitting some of the direct allusions to Fr. Bouyer's article.

represent a kind of esthetic compensation for much of the mediocrity we accept in thought and in action.   I believe that I am in accord with the intention of the author when I ask that, if the reader agrees with him rather than with me, he base that agreement on something other than this kind of satisfaction.

What would be an example of this kind of too ready agreement?   I would single out the danger of using in this debate the category of the "comfortable" and the category of the "uncompromising." Does there exist between Christianity and the world a possible synthesis or an irreducible antinomy? You may be in favor of the antinomy, and perhaps you are right.   But, before even entering into this difficult debate, simply note that if you propose the possibility of a synthesis, you offer to the mind that accepts it a "comfortable" solution of its doubts, but if you bring up your reasons against it as being so many "uncompromising considerations" you are likely, before any examination of the real issues, to attract many minds to your position.   For the public is so constituted that "uncompromising considerations" become literary successes; the most violent preachers are not those who are the least run after by the most worldly hearers.

In reality, "comfort" and "uncompromising-ness" seem to me, if not equally divided between the two camps, at least sought after by both the one and the other to a degree that has nothing to do with the moderation or the extremism of their theoretical positions.   The integrity of the faith, the zeal of charity, can on occasion throw the partisans of compromise into the most uncomfortable situations, far removed from the select circles where people sit about refining incisive paradoxes. Hippolytus of Rome, for example, calculating the margin of security that protected his flock from the end of the world, nevertheless interrupted his calculations with a prayer for martyrdom, [1] a prayer which seems to have been heard. [2]   A suburban pastor, filled with the "chimerical" hope of reconciling the Church with the modern world and, in order to realize this hope, thrown into a wearying life of fatigue and anxiety—should we say that he is trying to flee from difficulties? The effort of so many Christians of our generation, or of the preceding one, may include much illusion and call for many readjustments. All the same, it does not seem to me that we can immediately attribute it to a bargain-price Christianity or to a love of earthly things that has forgotten the one thing necessary.

It would be quite easy to turn various ironic statements back on their makers. But we might simply say that it is no more to the point to approve of a theological or apostolic attitude because it goes with the current of the world than to blame it because it does not go against this current. St. Paul tells Timothy to preach "in season and out of season" (2 Tim 4, 2). It seems that many of his modern exegetes cannot help choosing between

[1] *Commentaire sur Daniel*, II, xxx, ed. Bardy, pp. 166-7.
[2] If the Hippolytus of the *Commentary on Daniel* is actually the Roman martyr of that name.

them—some, the opportune truths and others, the inopportune ones. But a "dispenser of the mysteries of God" is not asked whether he has tried to charm or to shock his contemporaries: what is asked of him is "to be found faithful" (1 Cor 4, 2).

THE KINGDOM OF GOD AND THE WORLD

We may now go to the heart of the debate. I would like to state clearly where I can and where I cannot follow Fr. Bouyer.

The substance of agreement, the solid ground that can support our disagreements, is our common faith which provides them; and Fr. Bouyer has very opportunely recalled the various essential affirmations, too often forgotten, which must serve us here as a basis. It will be sufficient to enumerate them briefly:

1.   The Kingdom of God *transcends* the world. This means that the "Kingdom of God"—that is to say, the communication to men of a "salvation" which is participation in the life of God by knowledge and love—surpasses the "ontological" possibilities of this created world; that it is only made known to us by the "Good News" of Revelation; that it is only realized by the grace of God.

2.   The Kingdom of God encounters in the world the reality of *sin*. If it brings salvation, it is indeed the salvation of "what was lost," not

only a creature, but a sinful creature; and man enters into it only by a *conversion*. As to the sinful world, as such, not only is it not tending toward the Kingdom of God, but it is hostile to the Kingdom and fights against it.

3. The preparation, the foundation, the definitive establishment of the Kingdom of God have their history, which develops according to its own rhythm, and not according to the rhythms of the world and of "world history." The agent of the Kingdom of God is, in fact, none other than God Himself. The redemptive Incarnation gives time a new division and freely marks in the created world, against the sinful world, the moments of divine intervention: the choice of Israel, Easter, the Parousia. [3]

4. The task of the Church and of the Christian is to bear witness, in the world, to the Kingdom which is prepared and inaugurated through them. "In the world and not of this world," the Church and the Christian have first of all to proclaim the truth of the Gospel, for the salvation of the world and not for its temporal success.

These four points which I have rather coolly stated can be found, burning with evangelic boldness and polemic irony, in the glowing pages of Fr. Bouyer. Why detach them, why take them out of this perspective in which everything contributes

[3] See above, pp. 11-15, in relation to *Christ and Time*, by Cullmann.

to making them not only convincing but active, generating vital decisions? It is because this perspective seems to me to be quite one-sided here, and because the decisions to which it leads run the risk, as I see it, of entailing some ill-advised choices.

This perspective, I feel, results in the acknowledgment that between the world and the Kingdom of God, or between the world and the Church, there is "an insurmountable duality"—a formula which oversimplifies what I might call the mystery of the world, and which, seeming to take completely seriously, with a tragic seriousness, the fearful power for evil of created liberty, in reality suppresses it, by misunderstanding its roots in being. Contrary to the intention of the author, it seems to me that, for him also, "the die is cast"; it is cast in a different way, that is all.

As to the decision to which this leads, it amounts to assigning to the Church and to the Christian a role which in my opinion seems to be more that of a town crier than of a herald of good news. Having presented to the world, with the customary appeals, a solemn "take it or leave it," the Christian, the apostle, has nothing more to do with the world. He has only to cross it, like a camp or a field of battle, carrying the palm of martyrdom.

Have I misread my author? Let anyone who has read both of us be the judge. If I have, as it were, crystallized his positions, I have only done so in order to better formulate to myself, as I have understood them, the points on which I resist his line of thought. But I still need to explain my reasons for opposition; and I think that when I have done so we shall find that we have many convictions in common.

THE WORLD IN THE CHRISTIAN PERSPECTIVE

What is the world? Jesus said, "I have not come to judge the world, but to save the world" (Jn 12, 47); "I do not pray for the world" (Jn 17, 9). These statements, so clear and apparently so opposed to each other, oblige us, if we do not want to explain them away to the point of seeing no distinction between them, to recognize under the term "world," as it is used in Christian Revelation, a reality which is itself ambiguous.

Remaining in the perspective of our problem, let us try to clarify this ambiguity of the relations between the world and the Kingdom of God. We must here, it seems to me, distinguish in the very being of the world as it were a series of different answers to our questions.

1. The Bible opens with the account of creation. *The world is created by God*, and the God who created it found it very good (Gen 1, 31). This truth of Genesis was not forgotten either by St. John: "Without Him was made nothing that has been made" (Jn 1, 3), or by St. Paul: "He is before all things and all things hold together in Him" (Col 1, 17). Whatever "insurmountable duality" may seem to us to result from the later history of the world and of the Kingdom of God,

it cannot make us forget their common origin. And if we do not wish to reduce the act of creation to some "initial fillip," we must recognize that the very being of things and of men, their development and even the exercise of their freedom, are sustained and shot through and through by the Gift of God. "In Him we live and move and have our being" (Acts 17, 28). Let us then, in the rest of our analyses, beware of arriving at the point where, as St. Thomas Aquinas says: "To find fault with the perfection of creatures is to find fault with the Creator," [4] and of forgetting that in every creature, however sinful and lost it may be, there exists, as Claudel puts it (I quote from memory), "that sacred point in it that says *Pater Noster*."

2.   The world is not a disparate collection of inert figures, each fixed in its own nature. God at once crowned and coordinated His creation by the creation of spiritual beings and, moreover, for us men the world is *the world of man*, what man does in it and sees in it. [5]   This intervention of human liberty in order to affect the world becomes manifest to the believer to whom Scripture reveals a sinful world and a redeemed world; it finds its radical possibility in the created world as it came with man from the hands of God. The first account of Genesis charges man to "dominate the earth and subject it" (Gen 1, 28) and the second has him give

---

[4] On this point see L. B. Geiger, "L'existentialisme de Sartre et le salut chrétien," *Jeunesse de l'Eglise*, 7, especially pp. 80-82.

[5] "Detrahere ergo perfectioni creaturarum est detrahere perfectioni divinae virtutis" (*Contra Gentiles*, III, 69).

the animals their names (Gen 2, 19-20).   Things
therefore are not neutral with regard to man.
The knowledge that man gains about them, the use
that man makes of them, confer on them a practical
or speculative, ethical or aesthetic value, composing
from them a world, new worlds.   Certainly these are
not foreign to God's creation, for nothing that
exists or becomes escapes it, but in the hands of men
they are endowed with that life and freedom which
alone correspond fully with the intention of the
Creator. [6]   It is this total reality of the world
fashioned by the liberty of the spiritual creature that
we must now consider under the term "world."

3.   Now, created liberty is exercised, in fact,
in the direction of sin, and this world is a *sinful
world*.   The revelation of the fall follows, in Genesis,
immediately on that of creation.   St. Paul echoes
this: "By one man sin entered the world, and by
sin death" (Rom 5, 12), and this is not only a
collective but a cosmic enterprise: the whole of
creation finds itself "subject to vanity" (Rom 8, 20).
By the interplay of this dependence that we have
mentioned between the world and man, "the world"
is henceforth, according to St. John's meaning, the
cluster of rebellious liberties drawing with them into
their own imprisonment everything that ought
to find its completion in them: "Do not love the
world nor what is in the world... for everything

[6] Cf. St. Thomas Aquinas, *De veritate*, q. 11, a. 1: "God,
through the eminence of His will, confers on things, not only
their existence, but also their ability to act as causes."

in the world is concupiscence of the flesh, concupiscence of the eyes and the pride of life" (1 Jn 2, 15-16).

Is not the "insurmountable duality" which we just denied now brought about between such a "world" and the Kingdom of God? Does not denying it mean misunderstanding the depths of the "mystery of iniquity" and believing "not very seriously," as we are reproached with doing, in the Creator Himself by refusing to believe seriously in the fearful power that He has given to the liberty of His creatures?

I believe the opposite, and here we must set forth the chief cause of misunderstanding. For the "insurmountable duality" does not exist between the sinner and God nor between the sinful world and the Kingdom of God. Human freedom does not have the power to break with the Creator, by a decision which God would have only to "take note of," and to set up evil against Him as something henceforth independent. To say this would be to take away all reality from evil and from sin, and this opposition of the world would then be nothing but the opposition of a phantom. Evil is a reality, and nothing exists except what comes from the hands of God; between these fearful statements lies the mystery of a freedom that is bad—and yet created.

No, it is not, then, between the world, the work of this freedom, and the Kingdom of God that the abyss has been opened up. It is at the very heart of fallen freedom—and within the very order of creation—that a duality is located, "insurmountable" indeed by man who has caused it to arise, and unfathomable to human eyes. "Great is the wretchedness of man, not to be with Him without whom he cannot exist,"[7] so St. Augustine describes the state of sinful man. Evil, that irrefutable reality, does not *exist*. It can only locate its monstrous deficiency, its final nothingness, within what exists and what, existing, is of God: the world, man, freedom, the development of this world and the wishes of this liberty. Is this to make evil a mere "skin disease" and even less than this? But I would like to know how an evil could arise that would not be "on the surface," which would not be connected, with all its reality, to being—to the world which is the work of God.

Malum in bono. Indeed, if we take both good and evil and their irreducible opposition seriously, if we do not wish to neglect *any* of the scriptural texts, we must come back to this ancient Augustinian and Thomistic thesis. And its consequences for our debate can already be perceived. The world of sin is an enemy world, but, whatever it does, it is not a foreign world. In truth, the sinner enters and causes the world to enter with him into the "region of unlikeness," to use the wonderful phrase of St. Augustine. And it is there that salvation comes to seek him, to restore to him his lost unity—

[7] "Magna hominis miseria est cum illo non esse, sine quo non potest esse. In quo enim est procul dubio sine illo non est; et tamen si ejus non meminit, eumque non intelligit nec diligit, cum illo non est" (*De Trinitate*, VIV, XII, 16).

which God alone can restore. But it is there also, at each point of his divided being, at each crossroad of the world which leads him astray, that the preaching of the Gospel has a mission to proclaim salvation to him.

4. For the world is also a *redeemed world.* And the Redemption, which is the central mystery of our faith, must be understood not as a salvation which withdraws the elect from the world to cause them to enter into the mystery of God but, in truth, as the "salvation of the world."

We know that Christ our Savior has "overcome the world" (Jn 16, 33). We know also that He won this victory *in the world itself*: at Jerusalem, under Pontius Pilate, in our flesh. "The Word was made flesh and dwelt among us" (Jn 1, 14). It was by dying that He conquered death, it was by suffering abandonment by the Father that He reconciled men with God. Entering into the very heart of the sinful world, He destroyed its frightful adherence to evil. He untied the knot of wicked wills by the invasion of His merciful love.

This is why, as the new Adam (Rom 5, 12 ff.; 1 Cor 15, 22.45), He is the principle of a new world. To the world, the world of man become the sinful world, He offers the possibility of a new integration according to which the freedom of the sons of men—men become children of God—will fulfill even in the material order that "expectation of the creature" hitherto "subject to vanity" (Rom 8, 19-20). Such is the "Kingdom of God," the final response that the world—but the world transfigured—is to give to the question: What is the world?

> The earth is risen.
> It is the same.
> After the abyss of baptism...
> The same and yet new.
> The same and yet eternal. [8]

However, we are as yet given only the firstfruits of this new world: the Risen Christ. By His victory, Christ has set up in the world the powers of His Kingdom, but He has not yet established it. To use Cullmann's image, the decisive battle has been fought and won, but the "V Day" has not yet appeared when "all things will be made subject under His feet" (1 Cor 15, 25; Heb 10, 13; Acts 2, 34-35; Mt 22, 44; Mk 12, 36; Lk 20, 42) and the "last enemy, death" (1 Cor 15, 26) will be conquered. We remain in the sinful world, but it is henceforth a disunited world in which its contrary—the redeemed world—has now entered by the event of Easter as the possibility offered to our freedom.

It is essential to add that access to the Kingdom is not open to man and to the world by any way other than the one Christ opened up, that is, the Cross. This is true for each Christian and this is true for the world. Each Christian has still to "fill up what is lacking in the Passion of Christ" (Col 1, 24), to continue in his own flesh what Christ began in a decisive way in His own, that is, to transform "the world" which he bears within

---

[8] Paul Claudel, *La Cantate à trois voix*, at the end.

himself from a world of sin into a Kingdom of God. And "the world," the one in which he lives, will never cease to lay the wood of this cross on his shoulders.   Each Christian, we say; in this confusion of minor skirmishes, tramplings down and obscure sufferings, the coming of the Kingdom of God is lost sight of, it disappears from the world scene. But each combat is carried out "for His body which is the Church" (Col 1, 24), which is to grow "even to the ends of the earth" (Acts 1, 18; Rom 10, 18). The choice of one world or the other is carried out all through history until the day chosen by God when the return of the Lord, "revealing the intentions" of all men, will cause the redeemed world to rise from the heart of the sinful world.

THE GOOD NEWS PROCLAIMED TO THE WORLD

Thus "the world"—and the same must be said of "man"—appears to the eyes of the Christian in its unique reality as endowed with what I might call three levels of existence.   It is the created world constituted in its multiple nature, made up of determinisms and of freedoms, by the creative wisdom of God.   It is the sinful world such as it has been made by the guilty liberty of man.   It is the redeemed world as renewed by God's redemptive intervention (and this whether in the promise of Easter presented here and now by the Church, or in the final fulfillment of the Parousia).   Between these three levels two liberties are at work: the uncreated liberty of God, creative and redemptive; the created liberty of man, a sinner by his own defection and converted through the motion of grace.

It has been necessary to recall these theological points, and thus to summarize Fr. Bouyer's study in relation to a great number of them, in order to justify the position I oppose to his on the problem of the relationships between the Christian and the world.

The task of the Church, and the task of the Christian as such, is to proclaim to the world salvation by the Cross of Christ. But the complexity that I have just asked the reader to recognize in the Christian notion of "the world" seems to me to prohibit our oversimplifying the duty of proclaiming the Gospel.

How could the man who hears the Good News really hear it if the world to which he belongs is *only* the sinful world? It is because creation subsists beneath sin that communication remains possible and that the words of the tribe, those of its pride and its lusts, can receive and convey to his ears a new meaning. How could converted man be converted if the freedom that is his were *only* the "freedom" that he exercises for evil or that the world exercises for evil in his stead if, below this sinful liberty, beneath these poisoned waters that only grace can purify, there did not subsist inviolate the source of nature in which that liberty was born, intact in its first emerging as the creation of God, whose power sin itself bears witness to? But, if this is the way things are, to carry the Gospel to the world means by the word, for its free choice, through the grace of God, to reach that frontier where the sinful world adjoins the created world. If it is a question of saving and not of condemning, it is to this point where they can be heard that we must carry the call and also, I grant, the compelling summons.

The task of preaching, then, appears so "simple" that we shall never be done with it. Simple: we have nothing to proclaim other than what we have received, in its harsh simplicity; the apostles did not beat about the bush. It is not promised nor expected that the whole world will enthusiastically agree. But the whole world must *hear*, and we shall never finish with the task of bringing the word to the place where it is heard.

In order that the whole world may hear, we must therefore translate; and, after all, Christian preaching began with the miracle of tongues. But, after this encouraging miracle, the Holy Spirit has left us to grapple with these wearisome and thorny questions of translation. For along with words there are thoughts, "mentalities," cultures, "the world" and its way—which is also that of the devil. How can we reach the place where decisive choices are made and unmade, except by paths, sometimes direct and sometimes winding, which surmount continents and also "class-consciousnesses," geographical as well as ideological distances? And then—for the hungry belly has no ears—often those who are to hear you must first be given food...

And this is why I should like here to vindicate
all those efforts, however unskillful and however
unfortunate, on which Fr. Bouyer heaps irony, by
which so many "Constantinian" Christians, "medieval" Christians, "social-minded" Christians, etc.,
have tried to make the Gospel heard by the men of
their times, even to build a world in which the
Gospel could be heard.   Even if they have nourished
vain hopes of massive conversions or illusions of
"Christendom," these errors do not justify our
saying that such Christians have preferred the world
to Christ.   And if they have allowed their desire for
the imminent end to be somewhat dulled, at least
the Master, in coming to take them, will have
found them standing like "the faithful steward,
distributing (to the best of their ability) to each
his food" (Lk 12, 42 ff.), while they could have been
waiting for Him with their feet in their slippers
reading Léon Bloy.

No, it is not their breasts that I would have
beaten for our guilt.   Without adhering to their
"mystique of incarnation," we can, for all that,
learn from them the concrete care for this world
which our witness cannot do without.   You oppose
them with the parable of the wheat and the tares,
and doubtless this leaves nothing of some of their
illusions.   But have they not followed, after all,
His counsel not "to root up the tares before the time
for fear of rooting up the good grain also?"
Without rooting up the tares you rather seem
(forgive me) to be taking a furtive satisfaction in
noticing what fine fagots they will make in the final

furnace.   But the grain which may, here or there, grow hidden in the corners of the field that seem most abandoned to the foolish luxuriance of the weeds—is it not also worth some care?

AND THE PROFANE WORLD?

Must we go further and, having looked everywhere in the world for the men whom the Gospel must reach, acknowledge in the world itself, in the collective processes—if they exist and if they have a meaning—of its historical development, a value for the Kingdom of God?

This new question does not directly concern the Christian preaching which the New Testament clearly requires the apostles to bring *to men*.   But it does concern the Christian and the role which he must agree to refuse to play in the world.   Without pretending to solve the question here, I should like to try and clarify it, beyond what has been already said.

One point is certain: the advent of the Kingdom of God, a divinely initiated work, cannot be conditioned by any development of the world. Another point is no less certain: if such a development is in fact given and perceptible, we shall find in it, if freedom has any place in it, the marks that characterize a Christian view of the "world."   The created world and its development proceed from virtualities of nature, determined or free, the eventual deviations of which do not prevent us from hearing, as of everything that exists, the song of praise: "*All realities will sing; nothing else will.*"   The world of man, its total becoming, like its present state, will bear witness to the basic ambiguity of the works of its freedom.   In a world disfigured by sinful liberty, which has nonetheless lost, since Easter, its cohesiveness in sin, the successes of a true human progress—which the old wounds of liberty will always render precarious and the dominion of death relative—may alternate with the monstrous growth of a universe closed in on itself, through the gaps in which, however, the martyrs will still go forth.   Remote foreshadowings of the Kingdom may alternate with the shocking reminder of its transcendence.   The world can ripen like a fruit, and it can ripen like an abscess.   The game is not over.   I leave to the more knowledgeable the work of solving the enigma of the "millenium" of the Apocalypse, and the question: How will the world end?   I would be glad to answer with Fr. Gratry: "The world will end as it wishes," if I did not have to add at once: "The world will end as God wishes."

For both are true; this is the mystery of a freedom which is a created freedom.   And this is why, although he knows that the end is coming, it is not a matter of indifference to the Christian whether the world develops along one line or another, nor may he be indifferent, knowing his wretchedness, about fully being a man.   Far from turning away, as an indifferent or disgusted spectator, from the humble or the magnanimous efforts of men, he finds in his faith, as well as in the commandment of charity, reasons for playing his part on good days or bad, and for aiding his fellow men to sing the canticle of creation. And if one day, as is very likely, the world turns against him, he will, with " unwavering confidence," still think this canticle right. Since we have been reminded of the song of martyrs, we need only remember that the three young men in the fiery furnace found no better song to sing: "May all the works of the Lord bless the Lord."

CHAPTER III

St. Thomas Aquinas
and history *

It is a fact that "Scholasticism," including that of the
greatest of its representatives, St. Thomas Aquinas,
is of little interest to most Christians today, even
those most anxious to give a coherent intellectual
expression to their faith. It is also a fact that
clerics, whose seminary training demands their
initiation into Scholasticism, usually retain only
a certain number of "theses," precise and useful
formulations of Christian doctrine. They do not
find it to be the leaven capable of animating the
development of their religious thought, or organiz-
ing the reflections arising from their pastoral
experience. Once they have passed the final
examinations, they close their Scholastic manuals,
even the *Summa Theologica* itself, and never open
them again. Why?

Not necessarily because of intellectual laziness,
or contempt for theology, or carelessness about the

* These reflections in connection with the work of
M. D. Chenu, translated under the title *Toward Understanding
St. Thomas* (Chicago: Regnery, 1964), first appeared in *La vie
intellectuelle*, July 1951.

things of God. Nor even because their immediate activities use up all their energy. The tasks of the apostolic life are, to be sure, overwhelming. But it would seem as though, with very good young priests (and there are many), these tasks themselves would awaken a need for reflection, would even prove to be a call to contemplation, quite capable of evoking a theological renewal. Indeed, this renewal is already under way. Christian thought is always active. But the axis of this thought seems to have shifted since the not so remote time when "Neo-Thomism" aroused so many hopes and "Neo-Scholastic" reviews were founded.

Certainly, studies of this kind are being effectively carried on; but they do not seem to polarize the special interest and timely importance given them by large groups at the time of Cardinal Mercier. Today the same groups, and still larger ones, are led back beyond the reasoned developments of Christian thought toward what we might call in sum "the sources" of this thought: the Bible, the liturgy, the Fathers (and these considered less as makers of theological syntheses than as witness to living Tradition), and finally to the Church herself, whose concrete life seems rich in theological content. The greater part of the works which have appeared during the last twenty years in the Church arise from these orientations. These works both stimulate and echo the various "movements": the liturgical movement, the missionary movement, the biblical movement.

All this is well known and has even been

translated into tangible material form. Along with Missals, Bibles are multiplying. Pastoral problems are regularly the subject of publications and congresses. Even scholarly institutions, by nature slow to move, have been drawn in. Only twenty years ago, in seminaries and houses of study, biblical exegesis figured as "secondary matter" in relation to dogma and morals; it is doubtless too early to say that this is no longer true, yet this relationship tends to be reversed, or at least to become equalized. And the "history of salvation," in current catechesis, is again coming to take the place once reserved for it in the Paschal initiation of ancient times. On the other hand, the young seminarian often fails to grasp the relationship the "Scholastic philosophy" he learns might have to his apostolic desires. In the same way, the Christian who is instructed in his faith and seeks to understand it finds himself more at home, has the feeling of a closer harmony with his spiritual needs and the current of the Church's life, when he meditates on the texts and the actions of the liturgy, or makes direct contact with the Bible, than when he is introduced to the rational syntheses of theology.

HISTORY AND ITS MYSTERY

Is it possible to discover the *meaning* of these facts— about which we are as yet making no judgment? We might perhaps be allowed to do so by using a convenient formula, one already much used and abused.   It is a matter, if not of discovery, at least of a fruitful rediscovery of the *historical* character of Christianity; before it is a transcendent truth or an imperative norm, Christianity is a history.   From this fact comes the concrete, positive, existential character of the interest given it.   By the same token, "Scholasticism," the rational organization of the truths of Christianity—of the "eternal" truths—seems if not superfluous, at least secondary and rather lacking in reality.

It is easy to see that this view of things may be due to the environment in which the Christian lives today.   There is the concern for "efficiency" and the preoccupation, often very obvious, with proving to ourselves that Christian man, just as much as Marxist man, can flatter himself on going along "with the course of history."   There is the scientific vision of the world which has become dynamic and evolutionary.   And there is finally the modern concern for "authenticity," for the truth acquired rather than the truth " in itself. " [1]

But it would be false and unjust to see only this.   If the rediscovery of "historical" Christianity goes along the same lines as certain currents of modern thought, this cannot be merely the effect of a contamination of the faith by the modern world.

[1] So it is that, adopting this paradox of Lessing, Kierkegaard says: "If God held all truth firmly in His right hand and in His left the singular and ever-living drive toward the truth, and He said to me, 'Choose!' then, even at the risk of always and eternally deceiving myself, I should throw myself humbly on His left, and say: 'Father, grant me this.   The pure truth is surely for You alone.'" *(Postscript)*

It appears, rather, sometimes as the response *of this faith* to the world that is asking for it, and sometimes as the very *expression* that *the faith* is finding for itself, without any concern for what the world is doing.   And this is an authentic expression. Is not the Bible a "sacred history," and does not our Credo connect all time, from the Creation to the "life of the world to come," with what happened *sub Pontio Pilato?*   Does not living the liturgy make us continually "contemporary" with the event of Easter?   Does not the Church visibly appear to us to be a Church living in time, occupied with new generations to be born to grace, and with mysteriously preparing, through the movements of mankind, the "pleroma" of Christ?

However, whatever may be the present fortunes of this "historical" revaluation of Christianity and the echoes that it finds in many minds, whatever also may be its properly Christian justifications, we may ask ourselves whether it is perfectly clear about itself.   For, when all is said and done, what is " history?"   Does not this magical word, used today for such very different purposes, have many meanings which, if not opposed, are at least divergent?   We shall try to make a rapid inventory of some of these meanings.

1) To proclaim that "Christianity is primarily a history" is to say, in the first place, that Christian Revelation, before being formulated and set up as a body of doctrine, consists in a succession of *facts* (of the past and the eschatological future), a

collection of events, of acts of God and man, by which salvation "has come" and "is coming." It is, then, to insist on the gratuitous, sudden, irrational and irreversible character of Christian history, as of all history, and the impossibility of reducing it to any intuition and to any construction of the mind. For history is what excludes "ifs" and "buts"; it is what might have happened differently but happened as it did. Whatever the "causes" or the "laws" that can be found in it after the event, between these causes and laws and the *facts* (if it is a question of human facts, the only ones that are truly "historical"), there remains a certain free play, whether we call it chance or freedom—the freedom of man and the freedom of God.

2) But in the same affirmation: "Christianity is a history," the accent may be put differently—on the *unity* of that history. We forget the absolute newness of each of the events that constitute it in order to see only the thread that links them together, their internal dialectic, the plan of God which is developed here throughout time: now it is a question of a directed history, going toward an end. The Christian, instructed by St. Paul that there is a "mystery" at work in history, a "fullness of times," and a gestation of a new world, finds there a rich food for that hunger for synthesis which is elsewhere satisfied by "historical dialectics" of every kind. He then delightedly constructs a "theology of history" in which the biblical data are organized, often according to categories borrowed from an

evolutionary cosmology and sociology, and in which the hazards of liberty are lost to view in favor of a dynamic and optimistic vision of the march of redeemed humanity toward its goal.

3) These hazards are found again, but as it were interiorized and spiritualized when, repeating "Christianity is a history," we think of the "interior history" of each man with God, of the "movement" of conversion, of the *"itinerarium mentis ad Deum."* Then it is each Christian who, in faith, makes the Exodus and the Promised Land, Good Friday and Easter his own: it is his task to relive, to give this past history the life of interiority. In the Christian context, the accent this time is put on the spiritual event as opposed to the idea received; on the subjective character of the truth grasped by faith in opposition to its character of being given from without; on the ever-renewed dialogue with the God who speaks, in opposition to the dogmatic pronouncement which would be a truth always valid for all. So it is that Kierkegaard sought a truth which would be a truth *"for me,"* and the great problem as he saw it was not to integrate Christianity into "world history" but to *"become* Christian."

4) Finally, the perspectives, without ceasing to be real, can broaden. We then understand "Christianity is a history" in thinking of a history which is in the making, and collectively in the making. We give our attention not so much to the past event in the history of salvation, not so much

to its repetition in the interior movement of faith, not so much, finally, to the internal and infallible dialectic of the work of God in time, as to the "concrete situation" of each Christian generation and to the responsibilities which it must face *hic et nunc* in order to take in its turn its "place in history." The slogan, "we are the first Christians" is a fairly good expression of this conception.

It is not in order to oppose them, still less to refuse them altogether because of any such opposition, that we have tried to perceive, in the demand for historicity among modern Christians, these various currents which express equally different intellectual preoccupations and apostolic attitudes. On the contrary, we believe that they meet one another and are reconciled in the reality of Christian history as faith discovers it in the Bible, as the liturgy lives it, as the apostolic message of the Church proclaims it.

The liturgical celebration of the Paschal night, for example, has no meaning if it does not refer to the shocking and gratuitous fact of a certain tomb found empty, to the event of a certain night; "If Christ is not risen," says St. Paul, "our faith is vain." But neither would it have any meaning if this event of the past were shut in upon itself and unconnected with the centuries before and after it.   Finally, it would also be as empty as a celebration of July 14th—when no Bastille is taken—if nothing new were accomplished today, if those who participate in it did not thereby grasp the pledge of their own resurrection, each in the sanctuary of his redeemed liberty, and all together as the people of God on the march toward a victory which is only given to all.

But these aspects, both inseparable and contrasted, of Christian "history" show the extent to which it is a *mystery*, and what an alert faithfulness to it this mystery demands. To attach ourselves to the historical character of Christianity is, certainly, to go straight to the heart of the economy of salvation, and to return to a theological tradition which has Scripture itself as its starting-point: there is none more authentic. But it is also to raise many problems; and if we refuse to see them, do we not expose ourselves to the danger of unconsciously giving them a one-sided solution? We can easily see how each of the aspects of Christian history that we have distinguished, given our exclusive attention, runs the risk of ending up in a far-fetched conception which, by failing to integrate the complementary elements, finally compromises even that which it desires most to retain.

It can happen that the "return to the sources," for lack of exact analysis of the relations of the past and of the present, can be translated into an artificial way of acting, one that is falsely "primitive" and soon incapable of resisting the shocks of life. It can happen that the sense of Christian interiority changes into evasiveness. It can happen that the consideration of sacred history in its dynamic unity gives way to deceptive cosmological or sociological analogies in which the contemplation of the plan of God throughout history, for lack of attention to the twofold mystery of human freedom and divine freedom, ceases to be really a historical consideration and becomes a dialectic too sure of itself and, in short, another "scholasticism" in the place of the one that we wanted to do away with in the name of history. (And there is no worse scholasticism than one which does not know that it is one!)

Finally, at the end of all these deviations, it is not only this or that "ahistorical" element of Christianity that suffers from a too exclusive attention to history, it is history itself, history in its mystery, which disappears, leaving in the mind instead of itself a memory, or some texts, or a game, or a myth, or a dialectic, or an idea...

What are we to conclude, if not that a Christian thought anxious to be completely faithful to the historical character of the Christian datum cannot enclose itself in history, not even in a pure "theology of history." Certainly (to use the patristic categories), Revelation is carried out in an "economy": that is to say, in a historical dispensation of salvation, made up of divine and human actions, to which our own actions in time give us access; but this "economy" implies and calls for a "theology," that is to say, a revelation and a contemplation of the mystery of God Himself, [2]

---

[2] We therefore take these words "economy" and "theology" in the exact and full sense that *oikonomia* and *theologia* have in the Fathers; namely, *the historic dispensation of salvation*, and *the contemplation of the Mystery of God*. This will be their significance hereafter when they are cited, as here, in quotation marks. Otherwise, without quotation marks, they will have the looser and vaguer significance that is given them in common parlance.

the suprahistorical element without which *sacred history* would not exist—and would not be truly known. Why does this past contain the pledge of this future and command this present? Why does *a* history include in its dynamic unity the totality of all times, and how can this history be my history, concern me from its beginning to its end—if it were not that beyond history there is a God for whom "a thousand years are as a day" and if the Word of God incarnated in time did not participate in this eternity, to reign over all times?

It was not, therefore, out of idle curiosity that the first Christian centuries, bearers of the apostolic heritage and linked by the "chain of witnesses" to the *facts* of the history of salvation, were so concerned with searching the mysteries of God, and the great councils defined trinitarian and christological dogmas. No, it was not to "Hellenize" Christianity, it was to safeguard faith in the economy of salvation. Centuries before, when Moses was receiving a historical mission from God, he demanded to know His Name. In the same way, in order to assure faith in the works of God, we must discover in them the mystery of God which they reveal, and which gives them their meaning. [3]

The same problems, *mutatis mutandis*, arise today. After the undaunted efforts of the Fathers and the great medieval theologians to examine the Christian mysteries, theology became "scholastic"; catecheses followed it, and they seemed to rest on

---

[3] See above, the critique of Cullmann, pp. 25-39.

their acquisitions and to some extent to lose their contact with the "sources." Today, many minds have rediscovered this life-giving contact; but, in reaction, they are willing to believe that they need make no rational effort to assure it and organize it scientifically. Others, faithful adherents of a strongly conceptualized theology, view with apprehension this movement of a return to the Bible, to the liturgy, to a historical theology. Nonetheless, the same sovereign magisterium which declared, through the mouth of St. Pius X, that liturgical prayer is the "source of the Christian spirit" and so strongly recommended biblical studies in *Divino afflante Spiritu*, also recalled in *Humani generis* the present value of that Scholastic teaching which the Church has always maintained and without which a "return to the sources" would be deceptive.

Consequently, it is not a question of setting up two concurrent efforts against one another, of defending Scholastic theology *against* today's biblical and liturgical movements, or vice versa. The one needs the other. In our days also, a rediscovered "economy" needs to fructify in a "theology" in the deepest sense of the word, and this needs to assure and enlighten our study of the "economy." Our "sense of history" does not suffice of itself. To bear all its fruits, it calls for the complement of a properly theological understanding of history. This presupposes that between scholars and groups who are differently oriented, there will be, not only mutual respect, but also the resumption of a real dialogue. Is this not the condition of a renewal of Christian thought and one of the efforts which the Church has the right to expect from our generation?

ST. THOMAS AQUINAS, MASTER OF THE THEOLOGY OF HISTORY?

It may seem paradoxical to propose St. Thomas Aquinas as the master of this renewal, to ask him to stimulate and guide a Christian understanding of history. Is it not taken for granted that the Middle Ages were, among all Christian ages, those most lacking in the "sense of history?" Is not the theology of the great Scholastics, and of St. Thomas in particular, structured by a basically ahistorical thought, that of Aristotle, whose classification of human knowledge ignores history, whose logic, physics, and metaphysics are satisfied with definite notions, with immutable natures and atemporal essences, whose God is defined as "the first unmoved mover?" Did not a theology thus constructed leave in the background everything historical in Christian truth?

For all these reasons, various people have been tempted to consider the study of St. Thomas Aquinas, the study which the Church continues imperturbably to make the scaffolding and the basis of theological teaching, as unsuited to the present day—to see it as a scholarly survival which may have some pedagogical interest but cannot be very useful for living research and the progress of Christian thought. We are convinced that they are wrong. For, in reality, because it is Christian, the thought of St. Thomas remains historical, as does Christianity itself. And moreover, *precisely because it is rational*, because it "attacks" (in the chemical sense of the word) Christian truth by means of a reactor as powerfully ahistorical as Aristotelian thought, it actually results in a particularly lucid understanding of the irreducibly historical aspect of this truth; it clearly discerns the reality and the mystery of the Christian event. Its results, like its method, are therefore particularly valuable for us today.

These are the thoughts suggested by reading Fr. Chenu's admirable book, *Toward Understanding St. Thomas*. This work is termed the fruit of "continual teaching for more than twenty years." Those who have had the opportunity to benefit from this teaching know its exceptional quality; they know how the scholarly disciplines, an exact attention to the texts and their context, as well as doctrinal fidelity, are here made to serve a mind attentive to all the facts and all the tendencies of the life of the Church in our times. For Fr. Chenu, St. Thomas is not a text, but a master, the living master of a living disciple, each in love with the only truth. The disciple is a man of our times, engaged in our struggles. And also, through him, St. Thomas speaks to *us:* it is our own questions which he helps us not only to solve, but first of all to ask. Many others, with more authority, may doubtless testify along with us to having truly discovered the Bible as a result of this Thomistic teaching, and tell how, in a thought as carefully "structured" as that of the common Master, the fervor and probity of Fr. Chenu have enabled us to see the sources near at hand, the springing up of the living water. They will find again, in this book, the joy of these discoveries; and many others will here find a St. Thomas that they never knew before, not that great dead figure, the Angelic Doctor, canonized, set apart, respected and buried, but the master who is a brother to us who are alive today.

We shall not try to summarize this book here, but we shall bring out two themes very closely concerned with the problem of history.

THOMISTIC THOUGHT IN THE CONTEXT OF ITS OWN HISTORY

In the first place, even before looking to the thought of St. Thomas for the lights that it may give us *on* history, it is important for us to realize the extent to which this thought was itself a thought *within* history, in other words, a living thought. The majestic architecture of the great Thomistic works, the impersonal character of their methods of expression and reasoning, as well as the fact that they have become the possession of "the School," handed down as an inheritance from generation to generation, too readily make them seem a monument that stands detached from its author and its times, standing erect by virtue of its internal equilibrium, with the scaffolding needed to erect it long since removed. A monument of the past, some say, an "eternal" monument, others say; but in either case it no longer moves—it no longer lives. Yet, this

cathedral was planned. It was once in the process
of being constructed. To discover why and how
it was built is not mere archeological curiosity
that will add nothing to the understanding of the
"finished" work.

Fr. Chenu's *Toward Understanding St. Thomas* is,
first of all, such a historical introduction. Making
use of the many works (of Mandonnet, Grabmann,
Gilson, and those of Fr. Chenu himself and his
disciples) that have opened out the intellectual
history of the Middle Ages in the last fifty years,
it analyzes "the work in its environment," the
university setting of its development, the technical
and pedagogical procedures that it made use of, the
sources and means of documentation at its disposal,
and above all the historical needs that called it
forth. All this fills many pages which never allow
the reader to lose sight of the fact that the author
is concerned with the history *of a thought*. This
scholarship never lingers over one or other
Scholastic methods of teaching except to follow the
"life of the forms," as Foçillon would have said,
developed by a living thought. The objective
analysis of intellectual and spiritual currents meeting
in this thought only brings out more clearly the
uncertainty of the outcome of the grandeur and
freedom of the thought that managed to master
them. The whole work goes to prove the conviction
proclaimed at the outset that

> in their interplay and in their truth, and so in
> the understanding that we may gain of them,

the works of a genius and the humanity in which these works are rooted and bear their fruits beyond this same humanity, are closely identified with one another.

And Fr. Chenu adds:

Certainly, we believe with Carlyle in the primacy and the indispensability of personal genius—and St. Thomas is perhaps the most striking example of this—but we also know that the person is, to the extent to which he is a genius, one with the community, with the human communities in which this genius is planted. And we trust that, chapter by chapter, the reader will feel that he is growing in perception of the interior life of St. Thomas, to the extent to which he discovers in the background the social components of his thought, his work, his sources, his methods. To see a theological master come forth and labor, in an age in which theologians and theology were not separated from the world... this is a great sight, and a lesson for those who now see theology as exiled and jealous of its rights. It is needless to add that this consonance of theology with its own time in no way implies the relativism that some unperceptive persons have now and then concluded must belong to it. The truth is no less true because it is lodged in time.

THE THOMISTIC SYNTHESIS AND HISTORY

Thomist thought, then, *was* living at one time. But can it *still be* for us today a living thought with which we may hold a fruitful dialogue? Fr. Chenu's book strongly suggests a positive response that we shall try to clarify, starting from certain insights given in his work and remaining always in the perspective of the problem of history.

This problem, our problem, cannot but be found in the thought of St. Thomas to the very degree to which this thought is truly theological. Because it is so, Christian history cannot be absent from it. Fr. Chenu has very opportunely reminded us of the conditions of theological work in the thirteenth century: Holy Scripture remains the basic text, the object of the principal teaching of the master. But beyond this obligatory framework, we must recognize the fact that Scripture furnished the decisive inspirations for the developments of Thomistic theology which seem most purely rational.

> The biblical quotations which are strewn through his work are often merely decorative, as was the custom of his time; but the very substance of his labor is scriptural; his theology is basically born of evangelism, like the renaissance of which it is one of the effects... It is under the very pressure of the *auditus fidei*... that the *intellectus fidei* is begun and developed...

If we do not understand this fact, the thought of St. Thomas will certainly no longer be a living thought for us, for "the *Summa* is rooted in the soil of the Gospel," and "a tree cut off from its roots dies, even if it remains standing."

There is another discovery that we must make or make again in connection with the "Augustinianism" of St. Thomas.   Certainly, and this is obvious, his thought is opposed to that of St. Augustine clearly enough and consistently enough to preclude all concordance; it is therefore more suggestive to note the permanence of the great Augustinian themes in this theology, the rational structures of which, being of a wholly different type, too often capture the attention of commentators. These themes do not serve simply as a legacy from the past gathered out of respect for tradition, but as living elements, constantly reacting from within on the procedures of Aristotelian science in order to bend and sometimes even to reverse its meaning, by introducing a "history" into it. [4]

In fact, even if St. Thomas gives a different answer, he does not ignore any of the religious and Christian requirements with which the "committed" thought of St. Augustine confronted him.   He could not ignore them; Augustine's was *the* theology, for the Latin West of the twelfth century and the beginning of the thirteenth and still for St. Thomas himself. [5]   The way in which the original thought

[4] Thus the Augustinian view of "a concrete economy of man" in his "states" of innocence, of sin, of redemption, ends in transforming the abstract view of man into one involving "anthropology in the development of history and its sacred vicissitudes."   Thus, again, the rational eudaimonism inherited from Aristotle and the Augustinian dynamism of the quest for beatitude merge in the *Pars Secunda*, "where finality reigns religiously and where the theologal order, polarizing all asceticism, frees it from a rigid moralism."   These two examples from among many.

[5] Although he did not know the Greek Fathers well, and Dionysius, on the other hand, represents for him another important element of "Christian Platonism."

of St. Thomas gathered up this traditional heritage into a new synthesis illuminates the conditions of theological work in the Church: how the same faith can evoke theologies that are differently oriented, but also how the dialogue of these theologies is useful among themselves in order that they may not lose anything of the content of the faith. Here, the dialogue of St. Thomas with St. Augustine (who, in many respects, seems the closer to us) is valuable to us in that it assures us once again that Thomistic theology does not ignore the history of man as *viator*.

Thus, as scriptural and "Augustinian," in spite of the "rationalism" that it drew from Aristotle, the thought of St. Thomas remains subject, in the final analysis, to the Christian fact. This rules its whole interpretation. Strictness in reasoning is here put at the service of the movement of faith. With him "the intellectual man protects the spiritual man," Fr. Gardeil said. Fr. Chenu takes up this remark but gives it all its implications by completing it: "The spiritual element rules the intellectual. The intellectual, in turn, guards the spiritual." The most "rational" of all theologies remains a theology, a Christian system of thought—and so a "historical" thought...

But there is more to be said. To convince us of its contemporary interest it is not enough to know that the thought of St. Thomas "remains" the historical thought that preoccupies us. On the contrary, it is important for our purposes to show that St. Thomas brings a positive and original contribution to the development of this "historical" thought, that he actually *establishes* it with unequalled effectiveness. Here is, as we see it, the permanent and preeminently timely lesson of St. Thomas in connection with our problem. We find it precisely in the active confronting, through this thought, of the fact of Christian history with a method of rational organization to which this fact is apparently opposed. We find here, grasped in all its thorniness and masterfully coped with, the problem of the relationships between the "economy" and "theology."

The chapter that Fr. Chenu devotes to the *Summa Theologica* and, more precisely, to its plan, gives us valuable suggestions along this line. To write a "Summa," to give a rationally coherent exposition of Christian doctrine, to discover in it an *ordo disciplinae*, implies "the great problem of transforming a sacred history into an organized science." To the spontaneous historical order which follows the stages of the work of salvation (the order that we find in Hugh of St. Victor, for example) is opposed the notion of science accepted by Aristotle, which looks for logical and ontological connections, not chronological ones. "If there is a discipline which the Aristotelian method of classifying excludes from its orbit, it is certainly history." This science is in turn resisted by sacred history, woven "of contingent facts, works of the divine freedom and of human freedom, and consequently unconditioned in their existence and in their succession, irreducible to a series of reasons for their existence and to any chain of deductions."

Here is the problem. Sacred history presents us with *facts*. As such they are not subject to our reasoning, and human reason can only, in the last analysis, proclaim their "contingency," or else fall into illusion by substituting an "explanation" of its own making. Yet if the mind persists in looking for some intelligibility in history, it can only be found *beyond* history, in the mystery of God, of that divine freedom which, however contingent its works seem to us, and must seem, is nonetheless "the wisdom of God."

The course chosen by St. Thomas, his *ordo disciplinae*, clearly shows that in accepting history and its "contingency" without any hesitation, he nevertheless means to carry as far as possible the search for intelligibility, using all the resources of believing reason. We all know the plan which enabled him to do justice to these two apparently contradictory requirements: the Platonic theme of "emanation" and "return" around which the whole *Summa Theologica* is organized. But we must emphasize, following Fr. Chenu, the twofold advantage of this method. On the one hand, "the magnificent advantage of intelligibility: here every being, every action, every destiny, comes to be located, known, judged, in the very light of God. More than science, wisdom." And, on the other hand, "a plan open to history, to that sacred history the first page of which is precisely the description of the emanation of the world, the whole course of which is the divine governing of creatures, the fate of which is worked out by the works of men eager for blessedness, returning to God."

When the *Summa* is reread and studied in these perspectives, we discover it to be an instrument of great value in the development of a Christian "historical" thought.   The boldness in speculation and the strictness in reasoning inherited from Greek thought, because they are applied to the search for the first and last cause of all things, here become, for all that, eminently religious, "theological" in the best sense of the term.   They only seem to be abstracted from the concrete course of history because they go from the outset straight to the heart of history (of sacred history); this plan "tends *of itself* to lead theological wisdom beyond the economy which it is considering, to the divine reasons that rule it."   It resolves the "economy" in "theology"; it asks the God of Abraham, Isaac, and Jacob to reveal His Name.   What is sought in history is its "supreme suprahistoric intelligibility, by which theology is constituted as wisdom."

But we see, on the other hand, how this wisdom is respectful of history and of the resistance that history opposes to reason.   For to try to see all things *sub ratione Dei* is to renounce "rationalizing" these things, at any cost, to the measure of man— since one has from the first recognized that the mystery of God transcends our reason.   We must again and again renounce translating the intelligibility that we recognize in the wisdom of God into reasons convincing to us and allowing it to take on, so far as we are concerned, the name of "contingency"; the fearless search for necessary reasons will thus actually end in a more lucid recognition of the freedom that makes history.

Many characteristics of the *Summa* show this. It is thus, in the first place, that the Neo-Platonic schema of the *exitus* and the *reditus* was freed of the necessity which it originally possessed. *Christian* Neo-Platonism had already understood it in this way, before St. Thomas. No longer do the many proceed from the One by a necessary emanation, nor do the many return to the One by an idealistic dialectic. Each of the stages of the procession of beings from God or their return to God is henceforth marked, for our reason, with the sign of contingency and dominated, for faith, by the liberty of God. It is only at this price that we can say that the Platonic theme—and the plan of the *Summa*—is "open to history" and not to a mythical or idealistic appearance of history.

St. Thomas Aquinas uses it in this way very consciously. Creation is free, the call to beatitude is free, man's steps toward these are free, attentiveness to the need for grace is free, the redemptive Incarnation is free: so many breaks in the chain of necessary reasons. At the head of each of the corresponding treatises, the apodictic argument yields to the recognition of a *fact* for which the theologian can only respectfully propose "grounds of expediency." Fr. Chenu brings out the importance of "this very special type of intelligibility, gained by the theologian from the expedient argument (so looked down on in Aristotelian epistemology, but so essential to theological epistemology)." In fact, it marks the rational boldness of theological construction with the necessary sign of obedience to the revealed fact, and—if one may say so—with the sign of humor.

We must also bring out, it seems, the care with which St. Thomas allows for the possibility of these breaks in the interlinking of necessary causes, the precision with which he discerns in the order of nature the points at which liberty is inserted. The articles that he devotes to God's will, to Providence and to predestination, to human acts, to sin, to the problem of evil—which we are sometimes tempted to regard as purely speculative exercises—do no less than assure a precise intellectual grasp of what might be called the springs of history: man's freedom and God's freedom. We cannot develop this study here; in it, we believe, can be seen how the precise and quasi-biological analysis of the necessary appetite for the good leads to perceiving, at a quick glance, the mystery of liberty which Revelation as well as Christian experience imposes on theological reflection.

We must limit ourselves to these brief suggestions as to the role that history plays in the *Summa Theologica*. But they force us to attack one last point: the place given to Christ in this *Summa*.

Fr. Chenu brings up here "one of the most constant objections made to the plan of the *Summa* by certain modern theologians and spiritual writers, that theology is here completely constructed when

Christ enters on the scene." We know in fact that it is only after having finished, in an apparently complete and coherent way, in the *Pars Secunda*, the study of "the return of the reasonable creature to God" that St. Thomas begins a *Pars Tertia* to treat of Christ "inasmuch as He is for us, in His humanity, the way that allows us to tend toward God."

It is certain that the redeeming work of Christ constitutes the very center of the historical economy of Revelation; this is what gives meaning and unity to sacred history, and a theology which wishes to study the return of man to God in continuity with this concrete "economy" cannot dispense with the consideration of the Christian conditions of this return: how it has been accomplished once and for all in Christ and is accomplished in all ages by and with Christ. Must we see, in the tardy way in which this consideration is, as it were, "dragged in" in the *Summa*, proof that the sense of Christian history was lacking to St. Thomas? It seems to us that, on the contrary, this fact also testifies to this typically Thomistic attention to history that we have already mentioned: here history is encountered and, as it were, faced, but at the same time affirmed in what is irreducible in it, by the believing mind in search of the suprahistorical intelligibility which turns theology into wisdom.

The course adopted by St. Thomas putting outside the systematic study of the structures brought into play by the return of man to God the very "way" of this return, that is, the redeeming

Christ, only manifests the hard-core resistance which the fact of the Redemption opposes to all speculation that would "deduce" it from what God is or from what man is. This course radically accentuates the free and gratuitous character of the redeeming Incarnation, the "novelty" of the gift of God. Translating, in his plan, St. Thomas's thesis on the "reason for the Incarnation" as being not the masterpiece of God but the source of salvation, it marks, we might even say (at least in the framework of *this* plan), a "historical" reaction against a theology which would connect the mystery of Christ with the work of creation by abstracting it from the concrete history of sinful humanity.

Fr. Chenu expresses this in a formula which is vigorous, though perhaps ambiguous. What justifies St. Thomas's isolating the *Pars Tertia*, he says, is that if the Incarnation "constitutes the very substance of the economy... its first intelligibility nonetheless resides in its character of means." We might hesitate over using the term "means," since the expression "the very substance of the economy" which is here connected with it invites us to prefer the wider and more supple term "way" *(via)* which St. Thomas himself uses. In any case, we must surely not understand it in the sense that Christ is a means, among other possible ones God could have chosen to realize the redemptive purposes given at the outset; for He is *the* way, the "very substance of the economy"—outside of which nothing allows us to consider these divine ends as given.

We must therefore, with Fr. Chenu, deny the objection stated; no, theology is not "entirely constructed when Christ appears on the scene"; Christ is already taken into account when the *Pars Secunda* is developed, and without the revelation of Christ there would be no *Pars Secunda*. It refrains from naming Him as yet, because the inner logic of the *ordo disciplinae* requires that the study of these structures of grace still be pursued abstractly, even though their whole reality is Christian. But it goes forward to meet Christ, examining His gifts before recognizing Him in them, and it is from Him, in anticipation, that this search gains legitimacy and value. But theology is not "completely constructed" until it has met with Him. Alone, the *Pars Tertia* completes the *Summa;* it is its keystone; it marks the decisive encounter of "theology" and "economy." We believe that, through these last clarifications, we have come back to the very thought of Fr. Chenu which allows him to conclude by recognizing in the *Summa* "the fullness of the Gospel."

In approaching the end of this study, we do not mean to propose a pure and simple "return" to St. Thomas Aquinas, as if theology had come forth once and for all, fully armed, from this illustrious mind. If St. Thomas has contributed to setting up certain essential acquisitions of Christian thought, it remains no less true that today this thought finds itself facing new or renewed problems, either because the world has progressed or because the faith has lived on since the thirteenth century.

We should be poor Thomists if now we were to fall back on St. Thomas, leaving the answering of our problems to him. We must in our turn, by a collective effort, try to construct the living stones of the *Summa* of our times. In the face of new exigencies, this thought will always be born from the same "sources": the Word of God living in the Church, with our times calling for a new perception of it. But it is not a matter of indifference to us that in the development of these "sources" we should meet with a "master." A true master does not dispense truth ready-made. He teaches us to seek for it; he invites us to a dialogue. Our whole purpose has been to show that dialogue remains possible with him whom the Church recognizes as the common master, and that it can be fruitful.

CHAPTER IV

Toward a Christian vision of history

In connection with Teilhard de Chardin *

FROM THE "SUMMIT" TO THE "OMEGA POINT"

The work of Teilhard de Chardin is now generally recognized as of great importance. After having exercised widespread influence during the lifetime of its author, through semi-clandestine circulation, and having aroused in France, through posthumous publication, many controversies in Christian circles, it has now gained final status through foreign translations. In France itself, the noteworthy fact is the interest that certain intellectual communists have shown in it in their anxiety to maintain the

---

* This article appeared in *Signes du Temps*, July 1960.
   In addition to the works of Chardin himself, we would recommend reading the excellent *Introduction to the Thought of Teilhard de Chardin* by Claude Tresmontant (Baltimore: Helicon, 1963). In the present study, we are keeping to the perspective of "Physics" (or "Hyper-Physics") set out particularly in *The Phenomenon of Man* (New York: Harpers, 1961), in order to discover its consequences for the Christian meaning of history. It goes without saying that de Chardin's thought is broader: it includes a spirituality and a mysticism which cannot be reduced to this Physics. In the eyes of its author, *The Phenomenon of Man* is only a "phenomenological" approach to a total Christian vision of man and of history, a vision which necessarily depends on faith.

well-known "dialogue" they have already striven for in various other fields. The thinkers of the Party have even deemed de Chardin's work worthy of being called to the attention of the Soviet intelligentsia, speculating on whether it might not be well to translate *The Phenomenon of Man* into Russian. The question seems to be: Has the Omega Point taken the place of the Summit Conference as the meeting-ground for East and West?

Although much of this interest may merely be ephemeral (possibly inspired by ulterior, tactical motives) there is little reason for surprise at this, still less for discouragement. It is in the nature of things that Marxists, galvanized by a sense of history, theorists of and workers for a human progress that in their eyes demands communism for its basic condition, can hardly be indifferent to meeting with a Christian thinker who has issued from the citadel of dogma and has concerned himself with discovering the meaning of history—a man who finds both Faith and reason justifying a passionate preoccupation with the whole of human progress. A certain common language can therefore be utilized for the "dialogue." For his part, the Christian who is sure of his Faith cannot neglect any occasion or fail to run any risk of preaching before the altar of an "unknown god"—in this case, a "sense of history"—to those who would hear the news from there, but perhaps from nowhere else.

Naturally, the common language should not be full of ambiguities. There is no question that there exists a Christian view of history. But does the thought of Teilhard de Chardin give it exact and complete expression? And, on the basis of his thought, can we face the questions that are raised by those outside and give them a sound answer? These are the points on which we should like to make a few reflections here.

Is the history of man a chapter in the history of nature?

THE HISTORY OF MAN IN THE DEVELOPMENT OF THE WORLD

We have no intention of giving here a complete exposition of the vision of the world proposed by Teilhard de Chardin. We shall only bring in the elements which concern our purpose: the meaning of history. Teilhard de Chardin finds this meaning by integrating the human adventure into the development of the cosmos. Just as "the Catholic Church, driven into a corner by brigands, defends itself with the universe" (Claudel), so, according to this thinking, the hopes and the efforts of man, however precarious and lacking in order they may seem, find their justification, their measure, and their promise of victory in the fundamental law which directs the world in its totality.

This communication between historical man and the physical universe is only possible because the latter has already been recognized as itself being subject to development. The cosmos of the ancients was the realm of immobility or of eternal return: the circular movement of the stars, the succession of generations in fixed species. In the face of this unchangeable scene, the squabbles of gods and men were no more than futile games; as the song says, *"Les étoiles s'en foutent éperdument"* ("The stars couldn't care less"). But at least man, in the center of the world, occupied the foreground of the scene. Driven out by Galileo from this center and relegated to a chance planet, he saw his history radically separated from a nature in which he is only a negligible grain of dust in infinite space, a capricious accident in the constant interplay of universal laws.

For this image of a static or determined cosmos—which has no knowledge of human history—Teilhard de Chardin substitutes the perspectives of a "cosmogenesis." Through a bold generalizing of certain aspects of modern physics in which an irreversible trend appears (entropy, radioactivity, the "life" of atoms or stars), in geology (the "history" of the earth), and above all in biology and paleontology (the transformation of living species), the world no longer appears to the scientist's gaze as complete but rather as always being born; evolution is the major phenomenon in it; movement is not a perpetual beginning all over again but involves a real becoming. With this "becoming" of the world it will be possible to integrate the becoming of man.

The fact is that this becoming is directed, and Teilhard de Chardin perceives this direction in the "law of complexity-consciousness" which relocates man in the center of the world and makes him "the spearhead of evolution": "There exists, as a countercurrent to entropy, a cosmic drift of matter toward states that are more and more centro-complex... And self-consciousness presents itself experimentally as the *specific effect* of this complexity carried to extreme values."

Teilhard de Chardin adds: "If we apply this law of recurrence to the history of the world... we see sketched out a growing series of critical points and special developments."[1] Here we have one of the most original characteristics of his thought, the one which allows him to unify realms hitherto separated: evolution is not univocal; when a definite process of this evolution has developed all its consequences along the line of complexity-consciousness and can go no further, then its course is in some way taken over, once a certain "leap" has been made, by a new process of another order, and cosmogenesis continues on a higher level.

After the process that led from the atom to the most complicated chemical molecules, comes (after the "leap of life" has been made) the new process of phyletic evolution: the "biosphere" develops with all the ramifications of the tree of living things, of which the final spearhead is man. Man appeared (and having taken the "leap of thought"), his freedom in the "noosphere" takes up the relay and

[1] In *Un sommaire de ma Weltanschauung*, cited by C. Tresmontant in *Pierre Teilhard de Chardin: His Thought* (Baltimore: Helicon, 1959), p. 23.

extends the evolution of the cosmos, an evolution always as firmly oriented. To the eyes of the scientist, accustomed by the whole preceding history of the world to the vision of great wholes, the history of mankind evidences, through its incoherence and superficial struggles, a movement of convergence gathering men together, by a socialization which goes hand in hand with the conquest of a higher form of consciousness.

THE OMEGA POINT

Human history, our yet incomplete history, is therefore the front line of attack, the advance guard of cosmic evolution. But, as is clear, man only plays this determining role in the universe because he is organically linked with the universe, carried on by the same energies which led the evolution of the universe to man, and which are now manifested by the "socialization" of human efforts. Teilhard de Chardin recognizes that he made "two primordial options": "The first is the primacy given to psychics and to thought in the stuff of the universe. And the second is the 'biological' value attributed to the social fact taking place around us. The preeminent significance of man in nature, and the organic nature of mankind: two hypotheses... without which I do not see how a coherent and total representation of the phenomenon of man can be given." [2]

[2] *The Phenomenon of Man*, Eng. trans. Bernard Wall (New York: Harper, 1959).

But this integration of man in a totality that transcends him in no way implies, to Teilhard de Chardin, any subjection; on the contrary, it is a liberation. Evolution is an ascent toward spirit, and its perspectives come together with those of the Kingdom of God, in which God will be "all in all." If the evolution of the cosmos converges toward man, and if mankind itself converges toward a suprapersonal state, this double convergence postulates, according to Teilhard de Chardin, a "unique center in advance" in which mankind, and through mankind the world, will be gathered together. In this "omega point," the attraction of which alone explains the history of the world, Teilhard de Chardin recognizes the attributes of preexistence, of transcendence, and of universal recapitulation which are those of the "cosmic Christ" of St. Paul: "The firstborn of every creature... all things were created by Him and for Him" (Col 1, 15.17), and it is in expectation of His final manifestation, which will cause it to "enter into the freedom of the glory of the children of God" that "all creation groans in the pangs of birth until now" (Rom 8, 21-22).

CONSEQUENCES FOR CHRISTIAN ACTION

We can easily see the perspectives that this vision opens out to the Christian in the world. Eschatological expectation is no longer only the desire of personal hope—it expresses the vocation of the

world, inserted in its very nature; and the action
of the Christian in the world is thus "naturally"
connected with his eschatological hope, instead of
being contrary to it.   For the collective maturation
of humanity and human progress are ·actively
preparing for and hastening the "end of the world"
in the double sense of a temporal termination and of
a completion by perfection.

Far from scorning progress, detaching himself
from it and fleeing to the desert, the Christian will
collaborate wholeheartedly in the advancement of
things human.   In the struggles of history, he will
be in the forefront:

> We, the deserters?   We, mistrustful of the
> future of the physical world?   We, the men
> disgusted with human work?   Ah, how little
> you know of us!...   As if it were not for us,
> as much as and even more than for you, a
> question of life and death that the earth should
> succeed in the exercise of its natural powers!
> For you there is only the gain or setback of a
> reality which, envisioned even in terms of some
> kind of superhumanity, still remains vague
> and uncertain.   For us, it is a matter, in a true
> sense, of the triumphing of a God Himself...
> Like you, and indeed more than you (because
> it is I alone, of the two of us, who can extend
> to infinity, in accordance with the demands of
> my present will, the perspectives of my striving),
> I wish to devote myself, body and soul, to
> the sacred duty of the search.   Let us sound
> every depth, try every path, gaze into every
> abyss.   *Nihil intentatum* (let nothing be left

unprobed)... God wishes it, he who put all things in our care. You are a man? *Plus ego:* the more so, I. [3]

Man and his history

TOWARD A CRITICAL STUDY

In what we have said so far, we have tried to follow, freely but faithfully, Teilhard de Chardin's thought. The reader will have sensed, we hope, the magnanimity and the attractiveness of this open-air Christianity. We now need to test the firmness of its roots and of their attachment to the common faith.

To define our aims, we shall not examine here the value of Teilhard de Chardin's representation as a scientific vision of the world, nor the method used by this thought, in which analogy and extrapolation play a part that seems excessive to certain critics. Such an examination has been made. [4] Let us simply say that if various improprieties of vocabulary and method were pointed out and corrected, the whole method would seem legitimate to us, at least for sketching out a "working hypothesis."

[3] *The Divine Milieu,* Eng. trans. Bernard Wall (New York: Harper, 1960).
[4] See, on this matter, D, Dubarle, "A propos du phénomène humain," *La vie intellectuelle* (March, 1956), pp. 6-25, and the work of O. Rabut, *Dialogue avec Teilhard de Chardin* (Paris: Editions du Cerf, 1958).

Supposing that this value of the theory in itself has been accepted, it remains for us to verify how coherent it is with Christian revelation—its value as a Christian vision of the world and of history. Here again, we shall leave aside some important points, notably its relation to the doctrine of creation. Actually, this is not the major difficulty. Far from opposing biblical Revelation (as mechanistic evolution seemed to do), the directed evolution of Teilhard de Chardin "harmonizes" admirably with biblical thought (far better than the "eternal world" of Aristotle which St. Thomas had to accommodate himself to). [5] Indeed, it appears as "the expression of creation, in time and space, for our experience." In the same way, the representation given to the new creation, in which there appears (according to an image borrowed from Gregory of Nyssa contemplating the Savior coming out of the waters of the Jordan) "Christ streaming with the energies of the world in which He has immersed Himself"—this representation evokes in a very striking way a reign of Christ over the world which escapes all narrow jurisdiction and rejoins the depths of Paulinian theology.

Between creation and the new creation, the "in-between" of human history, and of sacred history, is what concerns us here. Does this

[5] We find illustrations of this accord, which Teilhard himself has not emphasized, in several works of Claude Tresmontant: *A Study of Hebrew Thought* (New York: Desclee, 1960); *Toward the Knowledge of God* (Baltimore: Helicon, 1961); *The Origins of Christian Philosophy* (New York: Hawthorn, 1963).

history allow itself to be included in the categories of Teilhard de Chardin's cosmogenesis? This is the whole question.

MAXWELL'S DEMON

Teilhard de Chardin has been reproached with having made light of human (and particularly of sinful) liberty. Is not the infallibility of evolution in its forward progress held in check by the appearance of man, who is capable of free choice and particularly of refusal? Cannot man, and sometimes a single man, change the course of history? And so it is useless to look for a meaning in history, and above all for the optimistic meaning of an infallible ascent toward higher being. This objection against Teilhard de Chardin does not seem to us to be a decisive one. But it may be useful to clarify it to see how, at least in principle, the play of liberty can be reconciled with a law governing the whole.

We have all heard of "Maxwell's demon" who intervenes in the explanation of the kinetic theory of gases. In a receptacle divided by a partition which is pierced with an opening, the pressure of gas is established at an identical mean density for the two sides: the rapid particles which cause high pressures, and slow particles which cause low pressures, both pass in either direction through the opening, and finally a statistical equilibrium is established. But if we were to equip the opening with a sliding door perfectly oiled, and suppose an agile and mischievous personage, our "demon," who took it into his head to manage the particles by opening and closing the door according to their direction and their speed, he would bring about the accumulation of rapid particles on one side and slow particles on the other, establish a difference in pressures, raise a potential, turn entropy about, upset physics by the caprice of his freedom.

In physics, "Maxwell's demon" is only a paradox, a professor's whim; he has no place in nature, where statistical determinism reigns uncontested. But we might willingly make him the genie of biological evolution as described by Teilhard de Chardin, directed toward the improbable and effective "against the current of entropy" in bringing about the most complex combinations, like Claudel's Prakriti trying out everything in her kitchen. At least this biological demon knows what he wants: to lead the series of beings along the line of complexity-consciousness. But does not the demon of human history (who may be called chance, freedom, or simply demon) introduce into the course of things a radical principle of indetermination? From Cleopatra's nose to de Gaulle's appeal for cooperation, the face of the world has changed many times; from the sin of Adam to the obedience of Abraham, the history of salvation has known revolts and conversions.

We said that this objection is not decisive. It seems to us, in fact, that the preceding considerations do not prevent us from seeking, and eventually finding, a meaning in history, and

seeing it as the last stage of a directed cosmogenesis.   They oblige us only to recognize the
proper character of the new process used by evolution in this new stage: it is *through* the interplay
of liberties and chances, with all that this includes
of the accidental and even the arbitrary, that the
ascent of the whole is carried out.   Contrary to
what a superficial reading of Teilhard de Chardin
might suggest, he did not misprize the accidents
of history, nor disasters, nor sin.   But he rightly
thought that these accidents did not in principle
prevent that "general drift" toward higher being, the
signs of which he believed he found in the
development of mankind.   The avatars of biological
evolution had already accustomed scientists to
discern basic necessity beneath chance.   He could
now sense in advance the victory which is being
prepared in the doubtful struggles of men.

It is enough, in order to justify this presentiment
(in principle if not in its expressed content), to
consent to the existence of structural laws, underly-
ing liberties, which infallibly orient the behavior
of the whole.   This is at least the working
hypothesis.   It remains legitimate; and the theologian can object to it least of all, since he teaches
a "divine government," mysteriously harmonized
with the interplay of the liberties that it infallibly
rules, and a *desiderium naturae* which remains
inscribed in the depths of fallen nature.   To discover,
even in human tasks, the surge of this desire which
can only be satisfied in the vision of God, is an
effort worthy of Christian hope.

The vision of the human adventure as a whole and the viewing of history as a stage in cosmogenesis, are therefore legitimate, at least in principle. But are they sufficient, and can we reduce history to cosmogenesis? That is the point.

IVAN AND ALYOSHA

The term "history" can be understood on different levels of reality, and we must explain on which of these levels we believe we are encountering what makes the true substance of history.

In the first place, "history" is one or another crude event that concerns a man, that concerns men. This event is obviously not an isolated one; it is located in a temporal and geographical setting, it has its ins and outs, it results from causes, from acts carried out previously, from external conditions or interior necessity, it is included (perhaps) in a law governing the whole; but first of all it is lived, for itself, once for all, by an existing man.

In the second place, "history" is the whole body of these facts, their successions in a certain time and their extension in a certain space—in brief what is recounted in history books, the wars of the Medes and the Persians, the communal movement in North Italy in the thirteenth century, etc. At this level we already find history having, we might say, different densities, going from the mere juxtaposition of facts with only a chronological relationship to the strict interlinking of events that lead on from one to the other according to an obvious causality.   History can have a small h or a capital H.

In truth, this transition from lower case to capital H and the choice of the type font in which to set the capital H of History depend largely on the intervention of the mind of the historian. [6]   And here is another level: the history of the historian, of historians (as there is the mechanics of Newton and that of Einstein).   At the top, we have the various "philosophies of history," attempts to bring together in a global unity the immense succession of human events.

History is all this.   As we have said, it is legitimate to take it at the second or the third level; nevertheless, the first cannot be forgotten.   An economic crisis, a famine, constitutes a coherent whole, one which is, in a certain way, intelligible; we can assign causes to it by giving it a capitalist or Marxist interpretation, and making it the starting point that will be ultimately beneficial for an examination of conscience and further progress. But this whole event cannot be totally abstracted from reality lived and experienced: in this or that lost village, a mother saw her child die of hunger. This is the substance of history.   If we forget this, we run the risk of misunderstanding the attitude (moral and practical) required of man and of the Christian with regard to history, his "historical task."   This attitude cannot be ruled by the vision of wholes alone.

[6] Cf. H. I. Marrou, "From the Logic of History to an Ethic for the Historian," *Cross Currents*, Vol. XI, No. I (Winter, 1961).

Here things work differently than at the anterior stages of "cosmogenesis": physical phenomena can be brought back to their law; biological and evolutionary facts are included in a series in which we can legitimately find their definitive intelligibility: the life and death of individuals, the transformation of species, have their *end* in this movement of the whole, the part is *for the sake of* the whole. But the human event has a unique substance. Certainly, it also enters into a whole; the "organic nature of mankind" can draw it along in this "general drift" toward the fullness of being which is to exalt the person himself. It remains true that this human cosmogenesis does not absorb, does not subsume historical reality as cosmogenesis in its preceding phases subsumes and sums up the activity of matter and the burgeoning of life. And consequently the happy result of this cosmogenesis cannot be the unique goal that must be assigned to man in history.

Remember the famous dialogue of the two brothers, Ivan and Alyosha in *The Brothers Karamazov.* [7] Ivan the rebellious is going to pour out to Alyosha, the mystic, the believer, the still candid novice, everything that he has been carrying in his heart. The basis of his rebellion is the problem of evil, particularly the suffering of the innocent. He does not refuse, he explains, to admit that this problem has a solution and that God will reveal it on the last day, but he estimates that the answer

[7] Eng. trans. Constance Garnett, Modern Library ed. pp. 229 ff.

is not *worth* the question, that there remains in the question something that the answer can never make up for: there is something in the tears of a child that universal harmony will not be enough to redeem, and if the tears of a child are necessary, even those of a child who will praise God on the last day, this is too high a price to pay for universal harmony.

> "I understand, of course, what an upheaval of the universe it will be, when everything in heaven and earth blends in one hymn of praise and everything that lives and has lived cries aloud: 'Thou art just, O Lord, for Thy ways are revealed.' When the mother embraces the fiend who threw her child to the dogs, and all three cry aloud with tears, 'Thou art just, O Lord!' then, of course, the crown of knowledge will be reached and all will be made clear. But what pulls me up here is that I can't accept that harmony. And while I am on earth, I make haste to take my own measures.... While there is still time, I hasten to protect myself and so I renounce the higher harmony altogether. It's not worth the tears of that one tortured child."

Alyosha has only a brief answer, but the decisive one. "Can you admit," Ivan asks him again, "the idea that men for whom you are building it would agree to accept their happiness on the foundation of the unexpiated blood of a little victim? And accepting it would remain happy for ever?"

"No, I can't admit it. Brother," said Alyosha suddenly..." you said just now, is there a being in the whole world who has the right to forgive and could forgive? But there is a Being and He can forgive everything, all and for all, because He gave His innocent blood for all and everything. You have forgotten Him, and on Him is built the edifice, and it is to Him they cry aloud, 'Thou art just, O Lord, for Thy ways are revealed!'"

GOD HIMSELF IS HISTORICAL AS WELL AS ETERNAL

The brothers' discussion then goed on to the celebrated "Legend of the Grand Inquisitor." But the essential point has been made. This gap between the fate of man and the universal harmony which we cannot bridge, the gap in which Ivan will always find the reason for refusing all five-year plans as well as all Christianities, this separation is only done away with by the blood of the Cross. Human history find its definitive unity only because there is a sacred history which crosses it with a streak of lightning and both consecrates it and makes it pertinent. Each of the events of human history takes on its definitive meaning in its mysterious relationship with the central and decisive event of this sacred history, the event of Easter. But this reconciliation, this recapitulation, are only possible because *God*, the Eternal One, has entered into history. "It was necessary that Christ suffer," that He "endure suffering" so that He could bear our sufferings: "*Vere languores nostros ipso tulit*" (Is 53, 4). But He had to be God so that His suffering, redemptive and victorious over death, should be present in the simultaneity, in the immanence of eternity to each redeemed suffering person: "I shed this drop of blood for you." It is because Christ, who died under Pontius Pilate and rose again, is seated at the right hand of God and "reigns forever and ever," that He is close enough to all innocents who suffer to truly "wipe away every tear from their eyes" (Is 35, 10; Apoc 21, 4).

To paraphrase Peguy: "God Himself is historical as well as eternal." It needed no one less than God to reconcile history and History, the personal destiny of "each of these little ones" and the progress of the world in the direction of the definitive Kingdom. The Christian cannot content himself with anything less than God, than the mystery of God, to justify his involvement in the tasks of this world. Otherwise Ivan would be right, and we should have to "give back our admission tickets."

QUASI NON UTENTES...

The Christian's attitude with regard to history, its tasks and its events, cannot therefore be a kind of human preliminary to a later assumption in faith. His attitude must be "theologal": "We all, with faces uncovered, reflecting as in a mirror the glory of the Lord..." (2 Cor 3, 18). No equivocation, interior or exterior, can be left as to the nature of our involvement. We are not dispensed from any human task; the program of Genesis, "Fill the earth and subdue it" (Gen 1, 28), is always in force. It is the task of redeemed man to rediscover in fallen nature the desire of unspoiled nature, and to make it tend, as far as he can, toward "the expectation of creation." But we know also that "this world as we see it is passing away" (1 Cor 7, 31). It has already passed away as soon as we are by the side of a suffering brother, for whom we can do nothing—all cosmogenetic business being suspended—but give him daily bread, claiming justice for him and crying out with him, "Come, Lord Jesus."

The Christian's attitude may seem disconcerting to the unbeliever: involved and disengaged, "using the world as if not using it" (1 Cor 7, 31), does he not take away with one hand what he seems to give with the other? Does he, or does he not, take history seriously?—Certainly, he is taking a difficult road, and he himself does not cease to compromise his message, through fear of the world or satisfaction with the world. But there is no other road for him; in the end, he can only find "the meaning of history" in his faith.

NY. 31. — Printed in Belgium by DESCLÉE & Cie, ÉDITEURS, S. A. Tournai. — 10.788